ANNOUNCING THE HAVERGAL EDITION
NOW IN PREPARATION FOR PUBLICATION

The edition of *The Complete Works of Frances Ridley Havergal* has five parts:

Volume I *Behold Your King:*
             The Complete Poetical Works of Frances Ridley Havergal

Volume II *Whose I Am and Whom I Serve:*
             Prose Works of Frances Ridley Havergal

Volume III *Loving Messages for the Little Ones:*
             Works for Children by Frances Ridley Havergal

Volume IV *Love for Love: Frances Ridley Havergal:*
             Memorials, Letters and Biographical Works

Volume V *Songs of Truth and Love:*
             Music by Frances Ridley Havergal and William Henry Havergal

David L. Chalkley, Editor   Dr. Glen T. Wegge, Music Editor

The Music of Frances Ridley Havergal by Glen T. Wegge, Ph.D.

This Companion Volume to the Havergal edition is a valuable presentation of F.R.H.'s extant scores. Except for a very few of her hymntunes published in hymnbooks, most or nearly all of F.R.H.'s scores have been very little—if any at all—seen, or even known of, for nearly a century. What a valuable body of music has been unknown for so long and is now made available to many. Dr. Wegge completed his Ph.D. in Music Theory at Indiana University at Bloomington, and his diligence and thoroughness in this volume are obvious. First an analysis of F.R.H.'s compositions is given, an essay that both addresses the most advanced musicians and also reaches those who are untrained in music; then all the extant scores that have been found are newly typeset, with complete texts for each score and extensive indices at the end of the book. This volume presents F.R.H.'s music in newly typeset scores diligently prepared by Dr. Wegge, and Volume V of the Havergal edition presents the scores in facsimile, the original 19th century scores. (The essay—a dissertation—analysing her scores is given the same both in this Companion Volume and in Volume V of the Havergal edition.)

    Dr. Wegge is also preparing all of these scores for publication in performance folio editions.

Wayside Chimes. May.

Love for love.

"We have known & believed the love that God hath to us." I John 4. 16

Knowing that the God on high,
　With a tender Father's grace,
Waits to hear your faintest cry,
　Waits to show a Father's face, —
Stay & think! oh should not you
Love this gracious Father too?

Knowing Christ was crucified, —
　Knowing that He loves you now
Just as much as when He died
　With the thorns upon His brow, —
Stay & think! oh should not you
Love this blessed Saviour too?

Knowing that the Spirit strives
　With your weary, wandering heart,
Who would change the restless lives,
　Pure & perfect peace impart, —
Stay & think! oh should not you
Love this loving Spirit too?

　　　　Frances Ridley Havergal

Fair copy autograph of "Love for Love" in F.R.H.'s handwriting. See page 96.

My Song Is Love Unknown.

A Collection of Christian Poems.

To the glory of God and the enrichment of His people.

"This is my Friend,
    In Whose sweet praise
    I all my days
    Could gladly spend."

(Samuel Crossman on Galatians 6:14, on page 11)

Taken from the Edition of *The Complete Works of Frances Ridley Havergal*.

David L. Chalkley, Editor   Dr. Glen T. Wegge, Associate Editor

ISBN 978-1-937236-61-8   Library of Congress: 2011919005

Book cover by Sherry Goodwin and David Carter.

This collection of Christian poems was originally prepared to be a section entitled "to fill up the leaf withal," at the end of Volume I (entitled *Behold Your King: The Complete Poetical Works of Frances Ridley Havergal*) of the five-volume edition of *The Complete Works of Frances Ridley Havergal.* There were several more pieces that were not included for lack of space, and surely there are several or many other poems of similar richness and benefit of which I am not aware: though this collection is not at all an exhaustive group, this has true gold, true worship, from Christ alone, to Him alone.

Because this was originally gathered and typeset for a different purpose, as a separate section of others' poems at the end of Frances Ridley Havergal's poems, eight by her have been added at the end. (How does one pick only eight poems from the treasure chest of her works?)

The title of this small book is the first line of the poem on Galatians 6:14 by Samuel Crossman, on page 11. That poem ends with these lines:

> "This is my Friend
> In Whose sweet praise
> I all my days
> Could gladly spend."

Thanks be to God for His indescribable gift to us in Christ.

David Chalkley

Eleven Poems by George Herbert

The Posy.

Let wits contest,
And with their words and posies windows fill:
Less than the least
Of all Thy mercies, is my posy still.

This on my ring,
This by my picture, in my book I write:
Whether I sing,
Or say, or dictate, this is my delight.

Invention rest,
Comparisons go play, wit use thy will:
Less than the least
Of all God's mercies, is my posy still.

George Herbert (1593–1633)

A posy from Him: "Lord Jesus Christ, please do Thy truth in me, because of Thyself alone."

A True Hymn.

My joy, my life, my crown!
My heart was meaning all the day,
Somewhat it fain would say,
And still it runneth mutt'ring up and down
With only this, *My joy, my life, my crown.*

Yet slight not these few words.
If truly said, they may take part
Among the best in art.
The fineness which a hymn or psalm affords,
Is, when the soul unto the lines accords.

He Who craves all the mind,
And all the soul, and strength, and time,

If the words only rhyme,
Justly complains, that somewhat is behind
To make his verse, or write a hymn in kind.

Whereas if th' heart be moved,
Although the verse be somewhat scant,
God doth supply the want,
As when th' heart says (sighing to be approved),
"*O could I love!*" and stops: God writeth, "*Loved.*"

Easter.

Rise, heart. Thy Lord is risen. Sing His praise
Without delays,
Who takes thee by the hand, that thou likewise
With Him mayst rise.
That, as His death calcined[1] thee to dust,
His life may make thee gold, and much more, just.

Awake, my lute, and struggle for thy part
With all thy art.
The cross taught all wood to resound His name,
Who bore the same.
His stretched sinews taught all strings, what key
Is best to celebrate this most high day.

Consort, both heart and lute, and twist a song
Pleasant and long.
Or since all music is but three parts vied
And multiplied,
O let Thy blessed Spirit bear a part,
And make up our defects with His sweet art.

I got me flowers to straw my way.
I got me boughs off many a tree.
But Thou wast up by break of day,
And brought'st Thy sweets along with Thee.

The Sun arising in the East,
Though He give light, and th' East perfume,
If they should offer to contest
With Thy arising, they presume.

---

[1] calcine: to reduce and change by heat

Can there be any day but this,
Though many suns to shine endeavour?
We count three hundred, but we miss:
There is but one, and that one ever.

The Holy Scriptures.

I.

Oh Book! infinite sweetness! let my heart
    Suck ev'ry letter, and a honey gain.
    Precious for any grief in any part,
To clear the breast, to mollify all pain.
Thou art all health, health thriving, till it make
    A full eternity. Thou art a mass
    Of strange delights, where we may wish and take.
Ladies, look here: this is the thankful glass,
That mends the looker's eyes. This is the well
    That washes what it shows. Who can endear
    Thy praise too much? Thou art heav'n's Lidger here,
Working against the states of death and hell.
    Thou art joy's handsel: heav'n lies flat in Thee,
    Subject to ev'ry mounter's bended knee.

II.

Oh that I knew how all Thy lights combine,
    And the configurations of their glory!
    Seeing not only how each verse doth shine,
But all the constellations of the story.
This verse marks that, and both do make a motion
    Unto a third, that ten leaves off doth lie.
    Then as dispersed herbs do watch a potion,
These three make up some Christian's destiny.
Such are Thy secrets, which my life makes good,
    And comments on Thee: for in ev'ry thing
    Thy words do find me out, and parallels bring,
And in another make me understood.
    Stars are poor books, and oftentimes do miss.
    This Book of stars lights to eternal bliss.

The Elixir.

Teach me, my God and King,
  In all things Thee to see,
And what I do in any thing,
  To do it as for Thee.

Not rudely, as a beast,
  To run into an action;
But still to make Thee prepossest,
  And give it His perfection.

A man that looks on glass,
  On it may stay his eye;
Or if he pleaseth, through it pass,
  And then the heav'n espy.

All may of Thee partake:
  Nothing can be so mean,
Which with his tincture (for Thy sake)
  Will not grow bright and clean.

A servant with this clause
  Makes drudgery divine:
Who sweeps a room, as for Thy laws,
  Makes that and th' action fine.

This is the famous stone
  That turneth all to gold:
For that which God doth touch and own
  Cannot for less be told.

Aaron.

Holiness on the head,
Light and perfections on the breast,
Harmonious bells below, raising the dead
To lead them unto life and rest.
Thus are true Aarons drest.

Profaneness in my head,
Defects and darkness in my breast,
A noise of passions ringing me for dead
Unto a place where is no rest,
Poor priest thus am I drest.

Only another head
I have, another heart and breast,
Another music, making live not dead,
Without Whom I could have no rest:
In Him I am well drest.

Christ is my only head,
My alone only heart and breast,
My only music, striking me ev'n dead;
That to the old man I may rest,
And be in Him new drest.

So holy in my head,
Perfect and light in my dear breast,
My doctrine tun'd by Christ (Who is not dead,
But lives in me while I do rest).
Come, people. Aaron's drest.

The Holdfast.

I threatened to observe the strict decree
Of my dear God with all my power and might.
But I was told by one, it could not be,
Yet I might trust in God to be my light.
Then will I trust, said I, in Him alone.
Nay, ev'n to trust in Him, was also His:
We must confess, that nothing is our own.
Then I confess that He my succour is.
But to have nought is ours, not to confess
That we have nought. I stood amaz'd at this,
Much troubled, till I heard a friend express,
That all things were more ours by being His.
What Adam had, and forfeited for all,
Christ keepeth now, Who cannot fail or fall.

Discipline.

Throw away Thy rod.
Throw away Thy wrath.
O my God,
Take the gentle path.

For my heart's desire
Unto Thine is bent.
I aspire
To a full consent.

Not a word or look
I affect to own,
But by book,
And Thy book alone.

Though I fail, I weep.
Though I halt in pace,
Yet I creep
To the throne of grace.

Then let wrath remove.
Love will do the deed.
For with love
Stony hearts will bleed.

Love is swift of foot.
Love's a man of war,
And can shoot,
And can hit from far.

Who can 'scape His bow?
That which wrought on Thee,
Brought Thee low,
Needs must work on me.

Throw away Thy rod.
Though man frailties hath,
Thou art God.
Throw away Thy wrath.

Judgement.

Almighty Judge, how shall poor sinners brook
                Thy dreadful look,
Able a heart of iron to appall
                When Thou shalt call
For ev'ry man's peculiar book?

What others mean to do I know not well,
                Yet I hear tell
That some will point Thee to leaves therein
                So void of sin
That they in merit shall excel.

But I resolve, when Thou shalt call for mine,
                That to decline
And thrust a Testament into Thy hand:
                Let that be scanned.
There thou shalt find my faults are Thine.

Love.[1]

Love bade me welcome, yet my soul drew back,
                Guilty of dust and sin.
But quick-eyed Love, observing me grow slack
                From my first entrance in,
Drew nearer to me, sweetly questioning
                If I lacked anything.

"A guest," I answered, "worthy to be here."
                Love said, "You shall be he."
"I, the unkind, ungrateful? Ah my dear,
                I cannot look on Thee."
Love took my hand and smiling did reply,
                "Who made the eyes but I?"

"Truth, Lord, but I have marred them. Let my shame
                Go where it doth deserve."
"And know you not?" says Love, "Who bore the blame?"
                "My dear, then I will serve."
"You must sit down," says Love, "and taste My meat."
                So I did sit and eat.

[1] The end of *The Temple.*

Eleven Poems by George Herbert in his volume *The Temple* released on his deathbed and published the same year, 1633

Nine Poems by Samuel Crossman

These nine poems were published alone, complete, as *The Young Man's Meditation, or Some Few Sacred Poems upon Select Subjects and Scriptures* by Samuel Crossman (1624?–1684), London, 1664. They were later published as the concluding section or appendix at the end of *The Young Man's Calling, or the Whole Duty of Youth* by Crossman, published in London, 1685, a prose treatise to young people to follow Christ, with examples of godly young people, these nine poems being at the end. These poems were reprinted in 1863 by D. Sedgwick.

The Gift.

If thou knewest the gift of God &c. John 4:10

1. This is the gift, Thy gift, oh Lord!
   The token of Thy dearest love:
   The orient jewel of Thy word,
   Sent down my thankfulness to prove.

2. Great is his gift in all men's eyes,
   Who give himself his friend to save.
   My Lord does more: for foes He dies.
   This gift no parallel may have.

3. Great is the gift, the Giver great.
   Both justly to a wonder rise.
   Thou giv'st Thy Lamb to Thine for meat,
   And for their sins a sacrifice.

4. But Lord! whilst Thou giv'st to Thine,
   Others arose to vie with Thee.
   The world and Satan did combine,
   And they would needs a giving be.

5. Satan sins' pleasure offered,
   And almost forc'd them upon me;
   But while they bloomed, they withered,
   And, Lord, Thy gift my choice shall be.

6. Then did the world it's gays present,
   And full[1] alluring cried, "See, see:
   Here's that may rather give content,"
   But, Lord, Thy gift my choice shall be.

7. These cannot give, they'd steal away
   From me my Heav'n, my heart from Thee.
   What e'er they offer, I'll say nay.
   Still, Lord, Thy gift my choice shall be.

[1] full – "fully, wholly"

All flesh is as grass, and all the goodliness thereof as the flower of the field. The grass withereth, the flower fadeth, but the Word of our God shall stand for ever. Isaiah 40:6,8

1. Welcome, sweet words. As 'tis most meet,
   We will you in our bosom hide.
   Sweet words for present, but most sweet
   Because for ever you abide.

2. All flesh is as the fading grass,
   The voice from heav'n to earth thus cried.
   The whole world's glory away doth pass,
   But, Lord, Thy words, they still abide.

3. Man speaks, but all his words are wind;
   They ebb and flow with time and tide,
   Fit emblems of his fickle mind,
   But, Lord, Thy words, they still abide.

4. Our selves sometimes stand promising
   Great things, while we by Thee are tried.
   Our blossoms fall, no fruit they bring,
   But Lord, Thy words, they still abide.

5. Bless'd words, dear Lord! no words like Thine.
   In darkness light through them is spied.[2]
   Till death, and after death, they shine.
   Then, Lord, e'en then Thy words abide.

6. These words the Lamb's sweet writings be
   Of love and dowry to His bride.
   Here may His saints their portion see,
   Portions which ever shall abide.

[2] spied or "espied" – "seen"

7. Welcome, sweet words, sweet words indeed.
Heaven's Agent here, to Heav'n our Guide.
What e'er is needless, these we need.
Lord, let these words with us abide.

Upon the fifth of November.

The archers have sorely grieved him, and shot at him, and hated him, but his bow abode in strength . . . . Genesis 49:23,24

1. This day allows Thy praises, Lord!
Our grateful hearts to Thee shall sing.
Our thankful lips, they shall record
Thine ancient loves, Eternal King!

2. Our land shall boast, the Holy One
My great Preserver is become.
My Friend my foes hath overthrown,
And made the pit they digged their tomb.

3. With Parthian bows the archers came;
Rome's poisonous oil on th'arrows shone.
Thy Turtle was the archers' aim.
"Shoot, shoot," says Satan, "all's our own."

4. Fond, foolish Rome, how dar'st[1] oppose
Whom God in His safe bosom lays?
Thy malice may itself disclose,
But frustrate, still shall turn to praise.

5. Thy crozier staff, thy triple crown,
Those engines of deceit and pride,
Thy purple robe, thy blaz'd renown,
The dust shall ever, ever hide.

6. Thy merchants shall thy fall lament,
Thy lovers all in sackcloth mourn,
While Heaven and Earth in one consent
Shall sing Amen, let Babylon burn.

7. Then Lord, Thy spouse, whose dropping eyes,
Whose sighs, whose sufferings prove her Thine,
Shall from her pensive sorrows rise
And as the Lamb's fair Bride shall shine.

[1] dar'st: darest

8. Sweet day, sweet day, when shall it be?
   Why stays my Lord? Dear Saviour, come.
   Thy mourning spouse cries after Thee.
   Stay with me, or take me home.

He was wounded for our transgressions, he was bruised for our iniquities; the chastisement of our peace was upon him, and with his stripes we are healed. Isaiah 53:3

1. Thus did the Prince of Life, thus He
   That could not die, e'en died for me.
   My thoughtful heart, Lord! shall arise
   And ponder these deep mysteries.

2. What means His death Who knew no sin?
   Or what my life who live therein?
   Mine was the debt, and death my due,
   Thou wast pleased Thy Son to sue.

3. Thou, Lord, wast pleased on Him to lay
   The debt, and He the price to pay.
   The gospel feasts, though sweet to me,
   Are th'emblems of His agony.

4. And oh, how great His sufferings were,
   Who th' wrath of God and man did bear!
   The Father then forsakes the Son,
   And creatures 'gainst their Maker run.

5. Judas betrays, disciples flee,
   Whilst Jews and Romans crucify.
   Hereat the sun furls up his light,
   And clothes the earth in sable night.[1]

6. The joyless stars e'en seemed to say,
   Israel hath quench'd the Lamp of day.
   The stubborn mountains, they lament;
   The rocks, they are asunder rent.

7. The graves their sealèd doors unclose;
   The dead awakened also arose.
   Th' amazed centurion, mourning, cries,
   Oh, 'tis the Son of God that dies.

[1] God Himself covers the sight. Matthew 27:45.

8. Thus these all labour to confess
   Thy Deity, Thy righteousness.
   Enough, dear Lord! these offer me
   Supports for th' utmost faith in Thee.

God forbid that I should glory save in the cross of our Lord Jesus Christ. Galatians 6:14

1. My song is love unknown,[1]
   My Saviour's love to me,
   Love to the loveless shown,
   That they might lovely be.
       O who am I,
       That for my sake
       My Lord should take
       Frail flesh and die?

2. He came from His blest throne,
   Salvation to bestow;
   But men made strange, and none
   The long'd for Christ would know.
       But oh! my Friend,
       My Friend indeed,
       Who at my need
       His life did spend.

3. Sometimes they strew His way
   And His sweet praises sing,
   Resounding all the day
   Hosannas to their King.
       Then "Crucify"
       Is all their breath,
       And for His death
       They thirst and cry.

4. Why? What hath my Lord done?
   What makes this rage and spite?
   He made the lame to run,
   He gave the blind their sight.
       Sweet injuries!
       Yet they are these
       Themselves displease
       And 'gainst Him rise.

5. They rise, and needs will[2] have
   My dear Lord made away.
   A murderer they save;
   The Prince of Life they slay.
       Yet willing He[3]
       To suff'ring goes,
       That He His foes
       From thence might free.

6. In life no house, no home,
   My Lord on earth might have;
   In death no friendly tomb,
   But what a stranger gave.
       What may I say?
       Heav'n was His home,
       But mine the tomb
       Wherein He lay.

7. Here might I stay and sing,
   No story so divine.
   Never was love, dear King!
   Never was grief like Thine.
       This is my Friend,
       In Whose sweet praise
       I all my days
       Could gladly spend.

[1] 2 Corinthians 9:15   [2] needs will – "must"   [3] willing: not Crossman's inaccurate word "cheerful"

The Pilgrim's Farewell to the World.

For here we have no continuing city, but we seek one to come. Hebrews 13:14

1. Farewell poor world, I must be gone.
   Thou art no home, no rest for me.
   I'll take my staff and travel on
   Till I a better world may see.

2. Why art thou loth, my heart? Oh why
   Dost thus recoil within my breast?
   Grieve not, but say farewell, and fly
   Unto the ark, my dove! There's rest.

3. I come, my Lord, a pilgrim's pace;
   Weary and weak, I slowly move;
   Longing but can't yet reach the place,
   The gladsome place of rest above.

4. I come, my Lord; the floods here rise,
   These troubled seas foam nought but mire.
   My dove back to my Bosom flies.[1]
   Farewell poor world. Heav'n's my desire.

5. "Stay, stay," said earth, "whither, fond one?"
   "Here's a fair world. What would'st thou have?"
   Fair world? Oh! no, thy beauty's gone.
   An heav'nly Canaan, Lord, I crave.

6. Thus the ancient travellers, thus they,
   Weary of earth, sighed after Thee.
   They're gone before. I may not stay
   Till I both them and Thee may see.

7. Put on, my soul, put on with speed.
   Though th' way be long, the end is sweet.
   Once more, poor world, farewell indeed.
   In leaving thee, my Lord I meet.

[1] John 13:23, Genesis 8:8–11; Christ is the ark of God.

Christ's future coming to judgement, the Christian's present meditation.

Behold he cometh with clouds, and every eye shall see him. Revelation 1:7

1. Behold! He comes, comes from on high,
   Like lightning through the flaming sky.
   The saint's desire, the sinner's fear.
   Behold that solemn day draws near.

2. He comes, Who unto judgement shall
   All flesh to His tribunal call.
   Methinks I see the burnish'd throne
   Whereon my Saviour sits alone.

3. Methinks I see at His right hand
   His smiling saints in triumph stand.
   Methinks I hear condemnèd ones
   Howling their never-dying groans.

4. Methinks I see e'en time expire,
   The heav'ns and earth on flaming fire.
   Think not, my soul! thyself to hide;
   Thou canst not 'scape, but shalt be tried.

5. Lo, here the book whence Justice reads
   Sentence on sinner's sinful deeds.
   Lo, here the Mercy Psalm wherein
   My Judge speaks pardon to my sin.

6. I tremble, Lord, yet I must say,
   This is my long'd-for wedding-day.
   My Bridegroom is my Sovereign Lord,
   My jointure[1] drawn in His fair word.

7. My mansion built by Him on high,
   Where I may rest eternally.
   Then come, my Lord! dear Saviour! come,
   And when Thou pleasest take me home.

Amen. Even so come, Lord Jesus,
come quickly.

---

[1] jointure – an act of joining, the state of being joined, union, marriage; jointress – a woman who has a legal jointure

The Resurrection.

Though after my skin worms destroy this body, yet in my flesh shall I see God. Job 19:26

1. My life's a shade; my days
    Apace to death decline.
    My Lord is life. He'll raise
    My dust again, e'en mine.
        Sweet truth to me!
        I shall arise
        And with these eyes
        My Saviour see.

2. My peaceful grave shall keep
    My bones till that sweet day.
    I wake from my long sleep,
    And leave my bed of clay.
        Sweet truth to me!
        I shall arise
        And with these eyes
        My Saviour see.

3. My Lord, His angels shall
    Their golden trumpets sound,
    At Whose most welcome call [1]
    My grave shall be unbound.
        Sweet truth to me! &c.

4. I said sometimes with tears,
    Ah me! I'm loth to die.
    Lord, silence Thou these fears.
    My life's with Thee on high.
        Sweet truth to me! &c.

5. What means my trembling heart
    To be thus shy of death?
    My life and I shan't [2] part,
    Though I resign my breath.
        Sweet truth to me! &c.

6. Then welcome, harmless grave;
    By thee to heav'n I'll go.
    My Lord, His death shall save
    Me from the flames below.
        Sweet truth to me!
        I shall arise
        And with these eyes
        My Saviour see.

[2] shan't – "shall not"

[1] John 11, 1 Corinthians 15

Heaven.

When shall I come and appear before God? Psalm 42:2

First Part

1. Sweet place, sweet place alone!
    The court of God most high.
    The Heav'n of Heav'ns, the Throne
    Of spotless Majesty!
        Oh happy place!
        When shall I be,
        My God! with Thee
        To see Thy face?

2. The stranger homeward bends
    And sigheth for his rest:
    Heav'n is my home, my friends
    Lodge there in Abraham's breast.
        Oh happy place!
        When shall I be,
        My God! with Thee
        To see Thy face?

3. Earth's but a sorry tent,
   Pitch'd but a few frail days,
   A short-leas'd tenement.
   Heav'n's still my song, my praise.
      Oh happy place! &c.

4. These lower rooms, these here
   Thou dost with roses pave,
   And circl'st with crystal clear:
   But Heav'n, oh! Heav'n I crave.
      Oh happy place! &c.

5. No tears from any eyes
   Drop in that holy choir,
   But death itself there dies,
   And sighs themselves expire.
      Oh happy place! &c.

6. There shall temptation cease.
   My frailties there shall end.
   There shall I rest in peace
   In th' arms of my best Friend.
      Oh happy place! &c.

Second Part

1. Jerusalem on high
   My song and city is;
   My home when e'er I die,
   The center of my bliss.
      Oh happy place!
      When shall I be,
      My God! with Thee
      To see Thy face?

2. Thy walls, sweet city! thine
   With pearls are garneshèd.
   Thy gates with praises shine;
   Thy streets with gold are spread.
      Oh happy place!
      When shall I be,
      My God! with Thee
      To see Thy face?

3. No sun by day shines there,
   No moon by silent night.
   Oh! no, these needless are.
   The Lamb's the city's light.
      Oh happy place! &c.

4. There dwells my Lord, my King,
   Judg'd here unfit to live.
   There angels to Him sing,
   And lowly homage give.
      Oh happy place! &c.

5. The patriarchs of old
   There from their travels cease.
   The prophets there behold
   Their long'd for Prince of Peace.
      Oh happy place! &c.

6. The Lamb's apostles there
   I shall with joy behold.
   The harpers I shall hear
   Harping on harps of gold.
      Oh happy place! &c.

7. The bleeding martyrs, they
   Within those courts are found,
   Clothed in pure array,
   Their fears with glory crown'd.
      Oh happy place! &c.

8. Ah me! Ah me! that I
   In Kedar's tents here stay.
   No place like this on high.
   Thither, Lord! guide my way.
      Oh happy place!
      When shall I be,
      My God! with Thee
      Thy face to see.

Nine Poems by Samuel Crossman
(1624?–1684)

As Weary Pilgrim.

As weary pilgrim, now at rest,
　Hugs with delight his silent nest,
His wasted limbs now lie full soft,
　That mirey steps have trodden oft,
Blesses himself to think upon
　His dangers past, and travails done.
The burning sun no more shall heat,
　Nor stormy rains on him shall beat.
The briars and thorns no more shall scratch,
　Nor hungry wolves at him shall catch.
He erring paths no more shall tread,
　Nor wild fruits eat instead of bread.
For waters cold he doth not long,
　For thirst no more shall parch his tongue.
No rugged stones his feet shall gall,
　Nor stumps nor rocks cause him to fall.
All cares and fears he bids farewell
　And means in safety now to dwell.
A pilgrim, I, on earth perplexed
　With sins, with cares and sorrows vexed,
By age and pains brought to decay,
　And my clay house mold'ring away.
O, how I long to be at rest
　And soar on high among the blest.
This body shall in silence sleep,
　Mine eyes no more shall ever weep,
No fainting fits shall me assail,
　Nor grinding pains my body frail.
With cares and fears ne'er cumb'red be,
　Nor losses know, nor sorrows see.
What though my flesh shall there consume,
　It is the bed Christ did perfume.
And when a few years shall be gone,
　This mortal shall be clothed upon.
A corrupt carcass down it lies,
　A glorious body it shall rise.
In weakness and dishonour sown,
　In power 'tis raised by Christ alone.
Then soul and body shall unite
　And of their Maker have the sight,
Such lasting joys shall there behold
　As ear ne'er heard nor tongue e'er told.

Lord, make me ready for that day,
    Then come, dear Bridegroom, come away.

              Anne Bradstreet (1612–1672)

Three Hymns by Thomas Ken

A Morning Hymn.

Awake, my soul, and with the sun
Thy daily stage of duty run;
Shake off dull sloth, and early rise
To pay thy morning sacrifice.

Redeem thy mis-spent time that's
    past;
Live this day, as if 't were thy last:
T' improve thy talent take due care;
'Gainst the great Day thyself prepare.

Let all thy converse be sincere,
Thy conscience as the noon-day clear;
Think how all-seeing God thy ways
And all thy secret thoughts surveys.

Influenc'd by the Light divine,
Let thy own light in good works shine:
Reflect all Heaven's propitious ways
In ardent love and cheerful praise.

Wake, and lift up thyself, my heart,
And with the angels bear thy part,
Who all night long unwearied sing
Glory to the Eternal King.

I wake, I wake, ye heavenly choir.
May your devotion me inspire,
That I like you my age may spend,
Like you may on my God attend.

May I like you in God delight,
Have all day long my God in sight,
Perform like you my Maker's will.
O may I never more do ill.

Had I your wings, to heaven I'd fly,
But God shall that defect supply,
And my soul wing'd with warm desire
Shall all day long to Heav'n aspire.

Glory to Thee Who safe hast kept
And hast refresh'd me while I slept.
Grant, Lord, when I from death shall wake,
I may of endless Light partake.

I would not wake nor rise again,
E'en Heav'n itself I would disdain,
Wer't not Thou there to be enjoy'd
And I in hymns to be employ'd.

Heav'n is, dear Lord, where e'er Thou art;
O never then from me depart,
For to my soul 'tis hell to be
But for one moment without Thee.

Lord, I my vows to Thee renew.
Scatter my sins as morning dew.
Guard my first springs of thought and will,
And with Thyself my spirit fill.

Direct, control, suggest this day
All I design, or do, or say,
That all my powers, with all their might,
In Thy sole glory may unite.

Praise God, from Whom all blessings flow.
Praise Him, all creatures here below.
Praise Him above, y' angelic host.
Praise Father, Son, and Holy Ghost.

An Evening Hymn.

Glory to Thee, my God, this night,
For all the blessings of the Light.
Keep me, O keep me, King of Kings,
Under Thine own almighty wings.

Forgive me, Lord, for Thy dear Son,
The ill that I this day have done,
That with the world, myself, and Thee,
I, e'er I sleep, at peace may be.

Teach me to live, that I may dread
The grave as little as my bed;
Teach me to die, that so I may
Triumphing rise at the last day.

O may my soul on Thee repose,
And with sweet sleep mine eye-lids close,
Sleep that shall me more vig'rous make,
To serve my God when I awake.

When in the night I sleepless lie,
My soul with heavenly thoughts supply.
Let no ill dreams disturb my rest,
No powers of darkness me molest.

Dull sleep—of sense me to deprive,
I am but half my days alive.
Thy faithful lovers, Lord, are griev'd
To lie so long of Thee bereaved.

But though sleep o'er my frailty reigns,
Let it not hold me long in chains;
And now and then let loose my heart,
Till it an Hallelujah dart.

The faster sleep the sense does bind,
The more unfetter'd is the mind;
O may my soul, from matter free,
Thy unveil'd Goodness waking see!

O when shall I in endless day
Forever chase dark sleep away,
And endless praise with th' heavenly choir,
Incessant sing, and never tire?

You my blest Guardian, whilst I sleep,
Close to my bed your vigils keep;
Divine Love into me instill,
Stop all the avenues of ill.

Thought to thought with my soul
    converse.
Celestial joys to me rehearse,
And in my stead all the night long
Sing to my God a grateful song.

Praise God, from Whom all blessings
    flow.
Praise Him, all creatures here below.
Praise Him above, y' angelic host.
Praise Father, Son, and Holy Ghost.

A Midnight Hymn.

Lord, now my sleep does me forsake.
The sole possession of me take.
Let no vain fancy me illude,
Not one impure desire intrude.

Blest angels! while we silent lie,
You Hallelujahs sing on high.

You, ever wakeful near the throne,
Prostrate, adore the Three in One.

I now awake do with you join
To praise our God in hymns divine.
With you in heav'n I hope to dwell
And bid the night and world farewell.

My soul, when I shake off this dust,
Lord, in Thy arms I will entrust.
O make me Thy peculiar care,
Some heav'nly mansion me prepare.

Give me a place at Thy saints' feet,
Or some fall'n angel's vacant seat;
I'll strive to sing as loud as they,
Who sit above in brighter day.

O may I always ready stand,
With my lamp burning in my hand;
May I in sight of heav'n rejoice,
When e'er I hear the Bridegroom's voice.

Glory to Thee in light array'd,
Who light Thy dwelling place hast made.
An immense ocean of bright beams
From Thy all-glorious Godhead streams.

The sun in its meridian height
Is very darkness in Thy sight.
My soul O lighten and enflame
With thought and love of Thy great Name.

Blest Jesu, Thou on heav'n intent
Whole nights hast in devotion spent;
But I, frail creature, soon am tired,
And all my zeal is soon expired.

My soul, how canst thou weary grow
Of antedating Heav'n below,
In sacred hymns, and Divine Love,
Which will eternal be above?

Shine on me, Lord. New life impart.
Fresh ardours kindle in my heart.
One ray of Thy all-quick'ning light
Dispels the sloth and clouds of night.

Lord, lest the tempter me surprise,
Watch over Thine own sacrifice.
All loose, all idle thoughts cast out,
And make my very dreams devout.

Praise God, from Whom all blessings flow.
Praise Him, all creatures here below.
Praise Him above, y' angelic host.
Praise Father, Son, and Holy Ghost.

Three Hymns by Thomas Ken (1637–1711), published in London, 1695

Two Poems by Sir Henry Wotton

A Hymn to My God in a Night of My Late Sickness.

O Thou great Power, in Whom I move,
For Whom I live, to Whom I die,
Behold me through Thy beams of love,
Whilst on this couch of tears I lye,
    And cleanse my sordid soul within
    By Thy Christ's blood, the bath of sin.

No hallowed oils, no grains I need,
No rags of saints, no purging fire:
One rosie drop from David's seed [1]
Was worlds of seas to quench Thine ire.
    O precious Ransom! which once paid,
    That *Consummatum est* [2] was said.

[1] The precious blood of Jesus Christ
[2] *Consummatum est*– Latin, "It is finished." John 19:30

And said by Him, That said no more,
But sealed it with His sacred breath.
Thou then, That hast dispung'd my score,
And dying, wast the death of death:
    Be to me now, on Thee I call,
    My life, my strength, my joy, my all.

D. O. M.[1]

Eternal Mover, Whose diffusèd glory,
    To show our grovelling reason what Thou art,
Unfolds itself in clouds of nature's story,
    Where man, Thy proudest creature, acts his part,
      Whom yet, alas, I know not why we call
      The world's contracted sum, the little all;

For what are we but lumps of walking clay?
    Why should we swell? whence should our spirits rise?
Are not brute beasts as strong, and birds as gay,—
    Trees longer lived, and creeping things as wise?[2]
      Only our souls were left an inward light,
      To feel our weakness, and confess Thy might.

Thou, then, our strength, Father of life and death,
    To Whom our thanks, our vows, ourselves we owe,
From me, Thy tenant of this fading breath,
    Accept those lines which from Thy goodness flow,
      And Thou, That wert Thy regal prophet's muse,
      Do not Thy praise in weaker strains refuse!

Let these poor notes ascend unto Thy throne,
    Where majesty doth sit with mercy crowned,
Where my Redeemer lives, in Whom alone
    The errors of my wandering life are drowned,
      Where all the choir of Heaven resound the same,
      That only Thine, Thine is the saving Name!

Well, then, my soul, joy in the midst of pain.
    Thy Christ, That conquered hell, shall from above
With greater triumph yet return again
    And conquer His own justice with His love,

---

[1] D. O. M. Deo. Optimo. Maximo. the Latin phrase, "To God, the Best, the Greatest."
[2] Proverbs 6:6 and 30:24–28.

Commanding earth and seas to render those
Unto His bliss, for whom He paid His woes.

Now I have done; now are my thoughts at peace,
And now my joys are stronger than my grief.
I feel those comforts, that shall never cease,
Future in hope, but present in belief.
Thy words are true, Thy promises just,
And Thou wilt find Thy dearly-bought in dust!

Two Poems by Sir Henry Wotton (1568–1639)

Psalm for Christmas Day.

Fairest of morning lights appear,
    Thou blest and gaudy[1] day,
On which was born our Saviour dear.
    Arise and come away!

This day prevents[2] His day of doom.[3]
    His mercy now is nigh.
The mighty God of Love is come,
    The Dayspring from on high.

Behold the great Creator makes
    Himself a house of clay;
A robe of virgin flesh He takes,
    Which He will wear for aye.

Hark, hark, the wise Eternal Word
    Like a weak infant cries:
In form of servant is the Lord,
    And God in cradle lies.

This wonder struck the world amazed;
    It shook the starry frame.
Squadrons of spirits stood and gazed,
    Then down in troops they came.

Glad shepherds ran to view this sight;
    A choir of angels sings;
And eastern sages with delight
    Adore the King of kings.

Join then, all hearts that are not stone,
    And all our voices prove,
To celebrate this Holy One,
    The God of peace and love.

Thomas Pestel (1584?–1659?)

[1] gaudy – "festive, glorious"
[2] prevents – "precedes"
[3] His day of doom – His hour, John 2:4, 12:27, 17:1, His sacrifice of Himself for ours sins,
2 Corinthians 5:21; also, His day of wrath, when He returns and judges the ungodly

Chanticleer.

All this night shrill chanticleer,
Day's proclaiming trumpeter,
    Claps his wings and loudly cries,
    "Mortals, mortals, wake and rise!"
        See a wonder—
        Heaven is under,
From the earth is risen a Sun,
Shines all night, though the day be done.

Wake, O earth, wake everything!
Wake and hear the joy I bring.
    Wake and joy, for all this night
    Heaven and every twinkling light,
        All amazing,
        Still stand gazing.
Angels, powers, and all that be:
Wake, and joy this Sun to see.

Hail, O Sun, O blessèd Light,
Sent into the world by night.
    Let Thy rays and heavenly powers
    Shine in these dark souls of ours;
        For most duly
        Thou art truly
God and man, we do confess.
Hail, O Sun of Righteousness!

William Austin (1587–1634)

Two Poems by Jeremy Taylor

A Prayer for Charity.

Full of mercy, full of love,
Look upon us from above,
    Thou Who taught'st the blind man's night
    To entertain a double light,—
Thine and the day's (and that Thine too);
The lame away his crutches threw;
    The parchèd crust of leprosy
    Returned unto its infancy;
The dumb amazèd was to hear
His own unchained tongue strike his ear;
    The powerful mercy did e'en chase
    The Devil from his usurped place,
Where Thou Thyself shouldst dwell, not he.

O let Thy love our pattern be;
    Let Thy mercy teach one brother
    To forgive and love another,

That copying Thy mercy here,
Thy goodness may hereafter rear
   Our souls unto Thy glory, when
   Our dust shall cease to be with men.
                         Amen.

A Meditation of Death.

Death, the old serpent's son,
   Thou hadst a sting once like thy sire,
   That carried hell, and ever-burning fire;
But those black days are done;
Thy foolish spite buried thy sting
   In the profound and wide
   Wound of our Saviour's side.
And so thou art become a tame and harmless thing,
   A thing we dare not fear
   Since we hear
That our triumphant God to punish thee,
For the affront thou didst Him on the tree,
   Hath snatched the keys of hell out of thy hand
   And made thee stand
A porter to the gate of life, thy mortal enemy.
   O Thou Who art that gate, command
      That he may, when we die
      And thither fly,
Let us in to the courts of heaven through Thee.
                  Allelujah.

Two Poems by Jeremy Taylor (1613–1667)

Casting all your care upon God, for He careth for you.

1 Peter 5:7.

Come, heavy souls, oppressed that are
With doubts, and fears, and carking[1] care.
Lay all your burthens[2] down, and see
Where's One that carried once a tree

---

[1] carking – "distressful," distressing, worrying, stressing   [2] burthens – burdens

Upon His back, and, which is more,
A heavier weight, your sins, He bore.
Think then how easily He can
Your sorrows bear that's God and Man.
Think too how willing He's to take
Your care on Him, Who for your sake
Sweat bloody drops, prayed, fasted, cried,
Was bound, scourged, mocked, and crucified.
He that so much for you did do,
Will do yet more, and care for you.

Thomas Washbourne (1606–1687)

The Gardener.

John 20:1–18 "She, supposing him to be the gardener, saith unto him . . . ."

Mary prevents [1] the day; she rose to weep
And see the bed where Jesus lay asleep.
She found out Whom she sought, but doth not know
Her Master's face, thinks He's the gardener now.
This gardener Eden's garden did compose,
For which the chiefest plants and flowers He chose.
He took great care to have sweet rivers run
To enrich the ground where He His work begun.
He is the gardener still, and knoweth how
To make the lilies and the roses grow.
He knows the time to set, when to remove
His living plants to make them better prove.
He hath His pruning knife, when we grow wild,
To tame our nature, and make us more mild:
He curbs His dearest children; when 'tis need,
He cuts His choicest vine and makes it bleed.
He weeds the poisonous herbs which clog the ground:
He knows the rotten hearts, He knows the sound.
The blessed virgin was the pleasant bower
This Gardener lodged in His appointed hour:
Before His birth His garden was the womb;
In death He in a garden chose His tomb.

Rowland Watkyns (1616?–1664)

[1] prevent: to go before, precede

Three Poems by Joseph Beaumont

The Garden.

The garden's quit with me: as yesterday
I walked in that, today that walks in me;
    Through all my memory
It sweetly wanders, and has found a way
   To make me honestly possess
    What still another's is.

Yet this gain's dainty sense doth gall my mind
With the remembrance of a bitter loss.
    Alas, how odd and cross
Are earth's delights, in which the soul can find
   No honey, but withal some sting
    To check the pleasing thing.

For now I'm haunted with the thought of that
Heav'n-planted garden, where felicitie
    Flourish'd on every tree.
Lost, lost it is; for at the guarded gate
   A flaming sword forbiddeth sin
    (That's I) to enter in.

O Paradise! when I was turned out,
Hadst Thou but kept the Serpent still within,
    My banishment had been
Less sad and dangerous: but round about
   This wide world runneth raging he
    To banish me from me:

I feel that through my soul he death hath shot;
And Thou, alas, hast locked up life's tree.
    O miserable me,
What help were left, had Jesus' pity not
   Show'd me another tree, which can
    Enliven dying man.

That tree, made fertile by His own dear blood;
And by His death with quick'ning virtue fraught.
    I now dread not the thought
Of barricado'd Eden, since as good
   A paradise I planted see
    On open Calvary.

A Morning Hymn.

What's this morn's bright eye to me?
If I see not Thine and Thee,
Fairer Jesu, in Whose face
All my Heaven is spread! Alas,
Still I grovel in dead night,
Whilst I want Thy living light;
Dreaming with wide open eyes
Fond fantastic vanities.
Shine, my only Day-Star, shine:
So mine eyes shall wake by Thine;
So the dreams I grope in now
To clear visions all shall grow;
So my day shall measur'd be
By Thy grace's clarity;
So shall I discern the path
Thy sweet law prescribed hath:
For Thy ways cannot be shown
By any light but by Thine own.

Three Poems by Joseph Beaumont
(1616–1699)

An Evening Hymn.

Never yet could careless sleep
On Love's watchful eyelid creep.
Never yet could gloomy night
Damp His eye's immortal light.
Love is His own day, and sees
Whatsoe'er Himself doth please.
Love His piercing look can dart
Thro' the shades of my dark heart,
And read plainer far than I
All the spots which there do lie.
Pardon then what Thou dost see,
Mighty Love, in wretched me.
Let the sweet wrath of Thy ray
Chide my sinful night to day,
To the blessed day of grace
Whose dear East smiles in Thy face.
So no powers of darkness shall
In this night my soul appall;
So shall I the sounder sleep,
'Cause my heart awake I keep,
Meekly waiting upon Thee,
Whilst Thou deign'st to watch for me.

When I survey the wondrous cross
On which the Prince of glory died,
My richest gain I count but loss,
And pour contempt on all my pride.

Forbid it, Lord, that I should boast,
Save in the death of Christ my God!
All the vain things that charm me most,
I sacrifice them to His blood.

See, from His head, His hands, His feet
Sorrow and love flow mingled down!
Did e'er such love and sorrow meet,
Or thorns compose so rich a crown?

Were the whole realm of nature mine,
That were a present far too small;
Love so amazing, so divine,
Demands my soul, my life, my all.

Isaac Watts (1674–1748)

Faith's review and expectations.

1 Chronicles 17:16, 17

Amazing grace! (how sweet the sound)
That saved a wretch like me!
I once was lost, but now am found,
Was blind, but now I see.

'Twas grace that taught my heart to fear,
And grace those fears relieved;
How precious did that grace appear,
The hour I first believed!

Through many dangers, toils and snares,
I have already come;
'Tis grace has brought me safe thus far,
And grace will lead me home.

The Lord has promised good to me,
His word my hope secures;
He will my shield and portion be,
As long as life endures.

Yes, when this flesh and heart shall fail
And mortal life shall cease;
I shall possess, within the veil,
A life of joy and peace.

The earth shall soon dissolve like snow,
The sun forbear to shine;
But God, who called me here below,
Will be forever mine.

John Newton, *Only Hymns*, 1779, Book 1, Hymn 41.

How sweet the name of Jesus sounds
    In a believer's ear.
It sooths his sorrows, heals his wounds,
    And drives away his fear.

It makes the wounded spirit whole,
    And calms the troubled breast;
'Tis manna to the hungry soul,
    And to the weary rest.

Dear name! the rock on which I build
    My shield and hiding place,
My never failing treas'ry filled
    With boundless stores of grace.

By Thee my prayers acceptance gain,
    Although with sin defiled;
Satan accuses me in vain,
    And I am own'd a Child.

Jesus! my Shepherd, Husband, Friend,
    My Prophet, Priest, and King;
My Lord, my Life, my Way, my End,
    Accept the praise I bring.

Weak is the effort of my heart,
    And cold my warmest thought,
But when I see Thee as Thou art,
    I'll praise Thee as I ought.

Till then I would Thy love proclaim
    With every fleeting breath;
And may the music of Thy name
    Refresh my soul in death.

John Newton (1725–1807)

There is a fountain filled with blood,
    Drawn from Immanuel's veins,
And sinners plunged beneath that flood
    Lose all their guilty stains.

The dying thief rejoiced to see
    That fountain in his day,
And there may I, though vile as he,
    Wash all my sins away.

I do believe, I will believe,
    That Jesus died for me!
That on the cross He shed His blood,
    From sin to set me free.

Dear dying Lamb! Thy precious blood
    Shall never lose its power,
Till all the ransomed church of God
    Be saved to sin no more.

E'er since by faith I saw the stream
   Thy flowing wounds supply,
Redeeming love has been my theme,
   And shall be till I die.

Then in a nobler, sweeter song
   I'll sing Thy power to save,
When this poor lisping, stammering tongue
   Lies silent in the grave.

Lord, I believe Thou hast prepared
   (Unworthy though I be)
For me a blood-bought, free reward,
   A golden harp for me.

'Tis strung and tuned for endless years,
   And formed by power divine,
To sound in God the Father's ears
   No other name than Thine.

William Cowper (1731–1800)

"Rock of Ages."

Rock of Ages, cleft for me,
Let me hide myself in Thee!
Let the water and the blood
From Thy riven side which flow'd,
Be of sin the double cure,
Cleanse me from its guilt and power.

Not the labours of my hands
Can fulfil Thy law's demands;
Could my zeal no respite know,
Could my tears for ever flow,
All for sin could not atone;
Thou must save, and Thou alone.

Nothing in my hand I bring;
Simply to Thy Cross I cling;
Naked, come to Thee for dress;
Helpless, look to Thee for grace;
Foul, I to the Fountain fly;
Wash me, Saviour, or I die!

While I draw this fleeting breath,
When my eyelids close in death,
When I soar to worlds unknown,
See Thee on Thy judgement throne,
Rock of Ages, cleft for me,
Let me hide myself in Thee.

Augustus Montague Toplady (1740–1778)

"After the Death of My Dear Husband."

My God, to Thee I raise mine eyes;
Calm resignation I implore.
O let no murmuring thought arise,
But let me humbly still adore.

With meek submission may I bear
Each needful cross Thou shalt ordain;
Nor think my trials too severe,
Nor dare Thy justice to arraign.

For though mysterious now Thy ways
To erring mortals may appear,
Hereafter we Thy name shall praise
For all our keenest sufferings here.

Now, Lord, Thy needful aid afford,
Nor let me sink in deep despair;
Aid me to trust Thy sacred word
And find my sweetest comfort there.

Charlotte Richardson (born 1775)

I asked the Lord that I might grow
  In faith, and love, and every grace;
Might more of His salvation know,
  And seek more earnestly His face.

'Twas He who taught me thus to pray,
  And He, I trust, has answered prayer!
But it has been in such a way,
  As almost drove me to despair.

I hoped that in some favoured hour
  At once He'd answer my request;
And, by His love's constraining power,
  Subdue my sins, and give me rest.

Instead of this, He made me feel
  The hidden evils of my heart,
And let the angry pow'rs of hell
  Assault my soul in every part.

Yea more, with His own hand He seemed
  Intent to aggravate my woe;
Crossed all the fair designs I schemed,
  Blasted my gourds, and laid me low.

"Lord, why is this?" I trembling cried,
  "Wilt thou pursue Thy worm to death?"
"'Tis in this way," the Lord replied,
  "I answer prayer for grace and faith."

"These inward trials I employ,
  From self, and pride, to set thee free,
And break thy schemes of earthly joy,
  That thou may'st find thy all in Me!"

John Newton (1725–1807)

Majestic sweetness sits enthroned
  Upon the Saviour's brow;
His head with radiant glories crowned,
  His lips with grace o'erflow.

He saw me plunged in deep distress,
  He flew to my relief;
For me He bore the shameful cross,
  And carried all my grief.

To Him I owe my life and breath,
  And all the joys I have.
He makes me triumph over death,
  He saves me from the grave.

To heav'n, the place of His abode,
  He brings my weary feet;
Shows me the glories of my God,
  And makes my joys complete.

Since from His bounty I receive
  Such proofs of love divine,
Had I a thousand hearts to give,
  Lord, they should all be Thine.

Samuel Stennett (1727–1795)

Sola gratia.   By grace alone.
Sola fide.   By faith alone.
Sola Scriptura.   By Scripture alone.
Solus Christus.   Christ alone.
Soli Deo gloria.   Glory to God alone.

Jesus! and shall it ever be?
A mortal man ashamed of Thee!
Ashamed of Thee, whom angels praise,
Whose glories shine through endless days.

Ashamed of Jesus! sooner far
Let evening blush to own a star;
He sheds the beams of Light Divine
O'er this benighted soul of mine.

Ashamed of Jesus! just as soon
Let midnight be ashamed of noon:
'Tis midnight with my soul till He,
Bright Morning Star, bids darkness flee.

Ashamed of Jesus! that dear Friend
On Whom my hopes of heaven depend?
No! when I blush, be this my shame,
That I no more revere His name.

Ashamed of Jesus! yes I may,
When I've no guilt to wash away,
No tear to wipe, no good to crave,
No fears to quell, no soul to save.

Till then—nor is my boasting vain—
Till then I boast a Saviour slain:
And oh! may this my glory be,
That Christ is not ashamed of me!

Joseph Grigg, 1765; Benjamin Francis, 1787

Our blest Redeemer, ere he breathed
    His tender last farewell,
A Guide, a Comforter, bequeathed
    With us to dwell.

He comes, the mystic heavenly Dove,
    With sheltering wings outspread,
The holy balm of peace and love
    On earth to shed.

He comes, sweet influence to impart,
    A gracious, willing Guest,
Where He can find one humble heart
    Wherein to rest.

And His that gentle voice we hear,
    Soft as the breath of even,
That checks each fault, that calms each fear,
    And speaks of heaven.

And every virtue we possess,
    And every victory won,
And every thought of holiness,
    Are His alone.

Spirit of purity and grace,
    Our weakness, pitying, see:
O make our hearts Thy dwelling place
    And meet for Thee.

Henriette Auber (1773–1862)

Christian, dost thou see them on the holy ground?
How the troops of Midian prowl and prowl around?
Christian, up and smite them, counting gain but loss;
Smite them by the merit of the holy cross.

Christian, dost thou feel them, how they work within,
Striving, tempting, luring, goading into sin?

Christian, never tremble; never be downcast;
Gird thee for the battle, watch and pray and fast.

Christian, dost thou hear them, how they speak thee fair?
"Always fast and vigil? Always watch and prayer?"
Christian, answer boldly: "While I breathe, I pray!"
Peace shall follow battle, night shall end in day.

"Well I know thy trouble, O My servant true;
Thou art very weary, I was weary, too;
But that toil shall make thee some day all Mine own,
And the end of sorrow shall be near My throne."

John M. Neale (1818–1866)

There is a safe and secret place
    Beneath the wings divine,
Reserv'd for all the heirs of grace:
    Oh, be that refuge mine!

The least and feeblest there may bide
    Uninjur'd and unaw'd;
While thousands fall on every side,
    He rests secure in God.

The angels watch him on his way,
    And aid with friendly arm;
And Satan, roaring for his prey,
    May hate, but cannot harm.

He feeds in pastures large and fair
    Of love and truth divine;
O child of God, O glory's heir,
    How rich a lot is thine!

A hand almighty to defend,
    An ear for every call,
An honour'd life, a peaceful end,
    And heaven to crown it all!

Henry Francis Lyte (1793–1847)

O Lord, Thy wing outspread,
    And us Thy flock infold;
Thy broad wing spread, that coverèd
    Thy mercy-seat of old;
And o'er our nightly roof,
    And round our daily path,
Keep watch and ward, and hold aloof
    The devil and his wrath.

For Thou dost fence our head,
    And shield—yea, Thou alone—
The peasant on his pallet-bed,
    The prince upon his throne.
Make then our heart Thine ark,
    Whereon Thy Mystic Dove
May brood, and lighten it, when dark,
    With beams of peace and love.

That dearer far to Thee
　Than gold or cedar-shrine
The bodies of Thy saints may be,
　The souls by Thee made Thine.
So nevermore be stirr'd
　That voice within our heart,
The fearful word that once was heard,
　" Up, let us hence depart!"

William John Blew (1808–1894)

Four Poems by Christina Rossetti

Lord Jesus, who would think that I am Thine?
　Ah, who would think
Who sees me ready to turn back or sink,
　That Thou are mine?

I cannot hold Thee fast tho' Thou art mine:
　Hold Thou me fast,
So earth shall know at last and heaven at last
　That I am Thine.

A Better Resurrection.

I have no wit, no words, no tears;
　My heart within me like a stone
Is numbed too much for hopes or fears.
　Look right, look left, I dwell alone;
I lift mine eyes, but dimmed with grief
　No everlasting hills I see;
My life is in the falling leaf:
　O Jesus, quicken me.

My life is like a faded leaf,
　My harvest dwindled to a husk:
Truly my life is void and brief
　And tedious in the barren dusk;
My life is like a frozen thing,
　No bud nor greenness I can see;
Yet rise it shall—the sap of Spring;
　O Jesus, rise in me.

My life is like a broken bowl,
　A broken bowl that cannot hold
One drop of water for my soul
　Or cordial in the searching cold;
Cast in the fire the perished thing;
　Melt and remould it, till it be
A royal cup for Him, my King:
　O Jesus, drink of me.

Love Is Strong as Death.

"I have not sought Thee,
  I have not thirsted for Thee:
And now cold billows of death surround me,
Buffetting billows of death astound me,—
  Wilt Thou look upon, wilt Thou see
  Thy perishing me?"

"Yea, I have sought thee, yea, I have found thee,
  Yea, I have thirsted for thee,
Yea, long ago with love's bands I bound thee:
Now the Everlasting Arms surround thee,—
  Through death's darkness I look and see
  And clasp thee to Me."

None other Lamb, none other Name,
  None other Hope in heaven or earth or sea,
None other Hiding-place from guilt and shame,
  None beside Thee.

My faith burns low, my hope burns low,
  Only my heart's desire cries out in me
By the deep thunder of its want and woe,
  Cries out to Thee.

Lord, Thou art Life tho' I be dead,
  Love's Fire Thou art however cold I be:
Nor heaven have I, nor place to lay my head,
  Nor home, but Thee.

Four Poems by Christina Rossetti (1830–1894)

Sixteen Poems (and Ten Statements) by Robert Murray M'Cheyne

"Rose early to seek God and found Him Whom my soul loveth. Who would not rise
  early to meet such company?" [Journal: 23 February 1834]
"No amount of activity in the King's service will make up for the neglect of the King
  Himself."
"I hope and pray that it may be His will to restore me again to you and your parish,
  with a heart tutored by sickness to speak more and more as dying to dying."
"Speak to your people as on the brink of eternity."

"Live near to God, and so all things will appear to you little in comparison with eternal realities."

"If the veil of the world's machinery were lifted off, how much we would find is done in answer to the prayers of God's children."

"How many purposes God has in view of which we know nothing!"

"I earnestly long for more grace and personal holiness, and more usefulness."

"I feel there are two things it is impossible to desire with sufficient ardour—personal holiness, and the honour of Christ in the salvation of souls."

"Spared fig trees should bear much fruit; pray that it may be so with me."

(Ten Statements from *Memoir and Remains of the Rev. Robert Murray M'Cheyne*.)

The Barren Fig Tree.

Within a vineyard's sunny bound
An ample fig tree shelter found,
    Enjoying sun and showers—
The boughs were graceful to the view,
With spreading leaves of deep-green hue,
    And gaily blushing flowers.

When round the vintage season came,
The blooming fig was still the same,
    As promising and fair;
But though the leaves were broad and green,
No precious fruit was to be seen,
    Because no fruit was there.

"For three long years," the master cried,
"Fruit on this tree to find I've tried,
    But all in vain my toil;
Ungrateful tree! the axe's blow
Shall lay thy leafy honours low;
    Why cumbers it the soil?"

"Ah! let it stand just one year more,"
The dresser said, "till all my store
    Of rural arts I've shown;
About the massy roots I'll dig,
And if it bear, we've gained the fig—
    If not, then cut it down."

How many years hast thou, my heart,
Acted the barren fig tree's part,
    Leafy, and fresh, and fair,
Enjoying heavenly dews of grace,
And sunny smiles from God's own face—
    But where the fruit? ah! where?

How often must the Lord have prayed
That still my day might be delayed,
    Till all due means were tried;
Afflictions, mercies, health, and pain,
How long shall these be all in vain
    To teach this heart of pride?

Learn, O my soul, what God demands
Is not a faith like barren sands,
    But fruit of heavenly hue;
By this we prove that Christ we know,
If in His holy steps we go—
    Faith works by love, if true.

August 14, 1834.

Anoint mine eyes,
    O holy Dove!
That I may prize
    This book of love.

Unstop mine ear,
    Made deaf by sin,
That I may hear
    Thy voice within.

Break my hard heart,
    Jesus, my Lord;
In the inmost part
    Hide Thy sweet word.

Written in a Hebrew Bible that M'Cheyne gave to
a fellow-labourer in Dundee, Scotland.

My own loved Bible, must I part from thee,
Companion of my toils by land and sea;
Man of my counsels, soother of distress,
Guide of my steps through this world's wilderness!
In darkest nights, a lantern to my feet;
In gladsome days, as dropping honey sweet.
When first I parted from my quiet home,
At Thy command, for Israel's good to roam,
Thy gentle voice said, "For Jerusalem pray,
So shall Jehovah prosper all thy way."
When through the lonely wilderness we strayed,
Sighing in vain for palm-trees' cooling shade,
Thy words of comfort hushed each rising fear,
"The shadow of Thy mighty Rock is near."
And when we pitched our tents on Judah's hills,
Or thoughtful mused beside Siloa's rills;
Whene'er we climbed Mount Olivet, to gaze
Upon the sea, where stood in ancient days
The heaven-struck Sodom——
Sweet record of the past to faith's glad eyes,
Sweet promiser of glories yet to rise!

1839. Written by M'Cheyne after his Bible had been
dropped into Jacob's Well, while he was travelling in Israel.

"Thy word is a lamp unto my feet,
and a light unto my path."

When Israel knew not where to go,
God made the fiery pillar glow;
By night, by day, above the camp
It led the way—their guiding lamp:
Such is Thy holy word to me
In day of dark perplexity.
When devious paths before me spread,
And all invite my foot to tread,
I hear Thy voice behind me say—
"Believing soul, this is the way;
Walk thou in it." O gentle Dove,
How much Thy holy law I love!
      My lamp and light
      In the dark night.

When Paul amid the seas seemed lost,
By Adrian billows wildly tossed,
When neither sun nor star appeared,
And every wave its white head reared
Above the ship, beside his bed
An angel stood, and "Fear not" said.
Such is Thy holy word to me
When tossed upon affliction's sea:
When floods come in unto my soul,
And the deep waters o'er me roll,
With angel voice Thy word draws near
And says, " 'Tis I, why shouldst thou
    fear?
Through troubles great My saints must
    go
Into their rest, where neither woe
Nor sin can come; where every tear
From off the cheek shall disappear,
Wiped by God's hand." O gentle Dove,
Thy holy law how much I love!
      My lamp and light
      In the dark night.

When holy Stephen dauntless stood
Before the Jews, who sought his blood,
With angel face he looked on high,
And wondering, through the parted
    sky,
Saw Jesus risen from His throne
To claim the martyr as His own.
Angelic peace that sight bestowed,
With holy joy his bosom glowed;
And while the murderous stones they
    hurled,
His heaven-wrapt soul sought yonder
    world
Of rest. "My spirit, Saviour, keep,"
He cried, he kneeled, he fell asleep.
Such be Thy holy word to me
In hour of life's extremity!
Although no more the murdering hand
Is raised within our peaceful land—
The Church has rest, and I may ne'er
Be called the martyr's crown to wear:
Yet still, in whatsoever form
Death comes to me—in midnight
    storm
Whelming my bark, or in my nest,
Gently dismissing me to rest,—
O grant me in Thy word to see
A risen Saviour beckoning me.
No evil then my heart shall fear
In the dark valley. Thou art near!
My trembling soul and Thou, my
    God,
Alone are there; Thy staff and rod
Shall comfort me. O gentle Dove,
How much Thy holy law I love!
      My lamp and light
      In the dark night.

1838.

Jehovah Tsidkenu.

"The Lord our Righteousness"

(*The watchword of the Reformers.*)

I once was a stranger to grace and to God,
I knew not my danger, and felt not my load;
Though friends spoke in rapture of Christ on the tree,
Jehovah Tsidkenu was nothing to me.

I oft read with pleasure, to soothe or engage,
Isaiah's wild measure and John's simple page;
But e'en when they pictured the blood-sprinkled tree,
Jehovah Tsidkenu seemed nothing to me.

Like tears from the daughters of Zion that roll,
I wept when the waters went over His soul;
Yet thought not that my sins had nailed to the tree
Jehovah Tsidkenu—'twas nothing to me.

When free grace awoke me, by light from on high,
Then legal fears shook me, I trembled to die;
No refuge, no safety in self could I see—
Jehovah Tsidkenu my Saviour must be.

My terrors all vanished before the sweet name;
My guilty fears banished, with boldness I came
To drink at the fountain, life-giving and free—
Jehovah Tsidkenu is all things to me.

Jehovah Tsidkenu! my treasure and boast,
Jehovah Tsidkenu! I ne'er can be lost;
In thee I shall conquer by flood and by field—
My cable, my anchor, my breastplate and shield!

November 18, 1834.

Fountain of Siloam.

Isaiah 8:6.

Beneath Moriah's rocky side
  A gentle fountain springs;
Silent and soft its waters glide,
  Like the peace the Spirit brings.

The thirsty Arab stoops to drink
  Of the cool and quiet wave;
And the thirsty spirit stops to think
  Of Him Who came to save.

Siloam is the fountain's name,
  It means " ";
And thus the Holy Saviour's fame
  It gently spreads abroad.

O grant that I, like this sweet well,
  May Jesus' image bear,
And spend my life, my all, to tell
  How full His mercies are.

Foot of Carmel, Israel, June, 1839.

I will arise and seek my God,
And, bowed down beneath my load,
  Lay all my sins before Him;
Then He will wash my soul from sin,
And put a new heart me within,
  And teach me to adore Him.

O ye that fain would find the joy—
The only one that wants[1] alloy—
  Which never is deceiving;

Come to the Well of Life with me,
And drink, as it is proffered, free,
  The gospel draught receiving.

I come to Christ, because I know
The very worst are called to go;
  And when in faith I find Him,
I'll walk in Him, and lean on Him,
Because I cannot move a limb
  Until He say, " Unbind him."

[1] wants – lacks

June 30, 1832.

He tenderly binds up the broken in heart,
  The soul bowed down He will raise:
For mourning, the ointment of joy will impart:
  For heaviness, garments of praise.

Ah, come, then, and sing to the praise of our God,
  Who giveth and taketh away;
Who first by His kindness, and then by His rod,
  Would teach us, poor sinners, to pray.

For in the assembly of Jesus' first-born,
  Who anthems of gratitude raise,
Each heart has by great tribulation been torn,
  Each voice turned from wailing to praise.

November 24, 1834.

"I am debtor."

When this passing world is done,
When has sunk yon glaring sun,
When we stand with Christ in glory,
Looking o'er life's finished story,
Then, Lord, shall I fully know—
Not till then—how much I owe.

When I hear the wicked call
On the rocks and hills to fall,
When I see them start and shrink
On the fiery deluge brink,
Then, Lord, shall I fully know—
Not till then—how much I owe.

When I stand before the throne,
Dressed in beauty not my own,
When I see Thee as Thou art,
Love Thee with unsinning heart,
Then Lord, shall I fully know—
Not till then—how much I owe.

When the praise of heaven I hear,
Loud as thunders to the ear,
Loud as many waters' noise,
Sweet as harp's melodious voice,
Then, Lord, shall I fully know—
Not till then—how much I owe.

Even on earth, as through a glass
Darkly, let Thy glory pass,
Make forgiveness feel so sweet,
Make Thy Spirit's help so meet,
Even on earth, Lord, make me know
Something of how much I owe.

Chosen not for good in me,
Wakened up from wrath to flee,
Hidden in the Saviour's side,
By the Spirit sanctified,
Teach me, Lord, on earth to show,
By my love, how much I owe.

Oft I walk beneath the cloud,
Dark as midnight's gloomy shroud;
But, when fear is at the height,
Jesus comes, and all is light:
Blessed Jesus! bid me show
Doubting saints how much I owe.

When in flowery paths I tread,
Oft by sin I'm captive led;
Oft I fall, but still arise;
The Spirit comes—the tempter flies;
Blessed Spirit! bid me show
Weary sinners all I owe.

Oft the nights of sorrow reign—
Weeping, sickness, sighing, pain,
But a night Thine anger burns—
Morning comes, and joy returns:
God of comforts! bid me show
To Thy poor, how much I owe.

May, 1837.

Give me a man of God the truth to preach,
A house of prayer within convenient reach,
Seat-rents the poorest of the poor can pay,
A spot so small one pastor can survey:
Give these—and give the Spirit's genial shower,
Scotland shall be a garden all in flower!

[Written of the need for more churches in Scotland, "to bring to overgrown parishes the advantage of a faithful minister, placed over such a number of souls as he could really visit"—more laborers in the vineyard to reach those not reached.]

After Richard Baxter's *Call to the Unconverted.*

Though Baxter's lips have long in silence hung,
And death long hush'd that sinner-wakening tongue,

Yet still, though dead, he speaks aloud to all,
And from the grave still issues forth his "Call":
Like some loud angel-voice from Zion hill,
The mighty echo rolls and rumbles still.
Oh, grant that we, when sleeping in the dust,
May thus speak forth the wisdom of the just!

October, 1834.

Children Called to Christ.

Like mist on the mountain,
    Like ships on the sea,
So swiftly the years
    Of our pilgrimage flee;
In the grave of our fathers
    How soon we shall lie!
Dear children, to-day
    To a Saviour fly.

How sweet are the flowerets
    In April and May!
But often the frost makes
    Them wither away.
Like flowers you may fade:
    Are you ready to die?
While "yet there is room,"
    To a Saviour fly.

When Samuel was young,
    He first knew the Lord,
He slept in His smile
    And rejoiced in His word;
So most of God's children
    Are early brought nigh:
Oh, seek Him in youth—
    To a Saviour fly.

Do you ask me for pleasure?
    Then lean on His breast,
For there the sin-laden
    And weary find rest.
In the valley of death
    You will triumphing cry—
"If this is called dying,
    'Tis pleasant to die!"

January 1, 1837.

The Child Coming to Jesus.

Suffer me to come to Jesus,
    Mother, dear, forbid me not;
By His blood from hell He frees us,
    Makes us fair without a spot.

Suffer me, my earthly father,
    At His pierced feet to fall:
Why forbid me? help me, rather;
    Jesus is my all in all.

Suffer me to run unto Him:
    Gentle sisters, come with me.
Oh that all I love but knew Him!
    Then my home a heaven would be.

Loving playmates, gay and smiling,
    Bid me not forsake the cross;
Hard to bear is your reviling,
    Yet for Jesus all is dross.

Yes, though all the world have chid me,
    Father, mother, sister, friend—
Jesus never will forbid me!
      Jesus loves me to the end!

Gentle Shepherd, on Thy shoulder
    Carry me, a sinful lamb;
Give me faith, and make me bolder,
    Till with Thee in heaven I am.

July, 1841.

Peace be to thee, gentle boy!
Many years of health and joy!
Love your Bible more than play,
Grow in wisdom every day.
Like the lark on hovering wing,
Early rise, and mount and sing;
Like the dove that found no rest
Till it flew to Noah's breast,
Rest not in this world of sin,
Till the Saviour take thee in.

Written on the blank leaf of a book which M'Cheyne
sent to a little boy in his congregation.

"Peace to This House."

Long may peace within this dwelling
    Have its resting place;
Angel shields all harm repelling,—
    God, their God of grace.

May the dove-like Spirit guide them
    To the upright land!
May the Saviour-Shepherd feed them
    From His gentle hand!

Written of a home where he had been given a
pleasant retreat.

Oft as she taught the little maids of France
To leave the garland, castanet, and dance,
And listen to the words which she would say
About the crowns that never fade away,
A new expression kindled in her eye,
A holy brightness, borrowed from the sky.
And when, returning to her native land,
She bowed beneath a Father's chastening hand,
When the quick pulse and flush upon the cheek,
A touching warning to her friends would speak,

A holy cheerfulness yet filled her eye,
Willing she was to live, willing to die.
As the good Shunamite (the Scriptures tell),
When her son died, said meekly, " It is well,"
So when Sophia lost her infant boy,
And felt how dear-bought is a mother's joy,
When with green turf the little grave she spread,
" Not lost, but gone before," she meekly said.
And now they sleep together 'neath the willow,
The same dew drops upon their silent pillow.
Return, O mourner, from this double grave,
And praise the God Who all her graces gave.
Follow her faith, and let her mantle be
A cloak of holy zeal to cover thee.

> 1839. Written after hearing of the death of a
> friend, the wife of an English clergyman.

Sixteen Poems by Robert Murray M'Cheyne (1813–1843)

Fourteen Poems by Richard Wilton

Hymn to the Holy Spirit.

Come, Holy Dove,
Descend on silent pinion,
Brood o'er my sinful soul with patient love,
Till all my being owns Thy mild dominion.

Round yon sad Tree
With frequent circles hover,
That in my glorious Surety I may see
Grace to redeem and righteousness to cover.

On wings of peace
Bring from that precious Altar
The Blood which bids the storms of conscience cease,
And blots out all the debt of the defaulter.

Spirit of Grace,
Reveal in me my Saviour,
That I may gaze upon His mirrored Face,
Till I reflect it in my whole behaviour.

Oh, let me hear
Thy soft, low voice controlling
My devious steps with intimations clear,
With comforts manifold my heart consoling.

Let that sweet sound
To holy deeds allure me,
With heavenly echoes make my spirit bound,
And of my Home in Paradise assure me.

Come, Holy Dove,
Guide me to yon bright portal,
Where I shall see the Saviour Whom I love,
And enter on the joys which are immortal.

Snowdrops.

White thoughts we bring
Of waking Spring,
And happy bird
To music stirred.

Sweet thoughts we raise
Of those white days
When Mary mild
Presents her Child.

High thoughts we tell
With trembling bell—
Earth's Easter day,
Saints' white array.

Glad thoughts are ours
Of angel bowers,
Where sons of light
Shall walk in white.

[No two alike,
Each one unique,
Created by
Our Lord on high.

Sweet gifts from Him
Who made, sent them.
They Him declare
In silent air.

See in their white
His glory bright,
His wondrous love
He gently wove.

stanzas 5–7 by D.C.]

The Sparrow.

A sparrow lighted chirping on a spray
    Close to my window, as I knelt in prayer,
    Bowed by a heavy load of anxious care.
The morn was bitter, but the bird was gay,

And seemed by cheery look and chirp to say—
   What though the snow conceals my wonted fare,
   Nor have I barn or storehouse anywhere,
Yet I trust Heaven e'en on a winter's day.
That little bird came like a wingèd text,
   Fluttering from out God's Word to soothe my breast:
What though my life with wintry cares be vext,
   On a kind Father's watchful love I rest;
He meets this moment's need, I leave the next,
   And, always trusting, shall be always blest.

On My Highland Hare.

Without a care, and fondly prest
Upon my circling arm or breast,
   Peace beaming from its half-shut eye—
   No trouble known, no danger nigh—
My gentle favourite sinks to rest.

Ah, on its native mountain crest,
Could it have found a nook or nest,
   Where it might hear the storm rush by,
         Without a care?

Against our will we may be blest:
Let me not shrink or be distrest
   If cloud of change o'erspread my sky;
   It is God's shadowing Hand, and I
Will let Love choose what Love deems best,
         Without a care.

A Lesson of Trust.

I learn to trust from this dear Highland Hare,
   Which lays its gentle head upon my arm,
   And dozes on my knee without alarm,
As if it slumbered in its native lair.
Far from its heathery home and mountain air—
   How comes it that it never dreams of harm?
   What has subdued its fear? What potent charm
Commands this confidence so sweet and rare?

Love, true and constant, is the only spell;
    Kindness of act and feeling, voice and eye,
Has won its timorous heart to trust me well:
    Nor will I doubt *my* Benefactor high,
Whose kindnesses are more than I can tell,
    But trustful on His loving arm will lie.

Holy Scripture.

I have a garden fair,
    With Heavenly breezes fanned,
And every morning finds me there—
    It is the Lord's command—
To gather fruits and blossoms sweet
Before the dusty world I meet.

I have a faithful Friend,
    Accustomed to advise,
With Whom each morn some time I
        spend—
    That I may be made wise
To find and keep the only way
Which issues in eternal day.

I have an armoury bright,
    With shield and helm hung round,
Where, duly as the morning light,
    The Spirit's sword is found,
With which to overcome the foe
Who harasses the way I go.

I have a mirror keen
    Which shows me all I am;
But lo! behind me there is seen
    One like a dying Lamb;
And as I view His imaged Face,
My sins are lost in shining grace.

Oh, send Thy Spirit, Lord,
    To make me wholly Thine,
That I may love Thy blessèd Word,
    And feel its power divine,
And walk on calmly in its light
Till faith is turned to glorious sight.

Christmas Day.

In vesture white[1] the Eternal Child
Lay on His mother's lap and smiled:
    What joy to see that longed-for sight—
    Her spotless lily of delight!
Her love, her dove, her undefiled!

She reck'd not of the anguish wild,
The sorrow upon sorrow piled,
    His dead Form swathed, one awful night,
        In vesture white.[2]

Oh! let our hearts, this Birthday bright,
The sorrow and the joy unite;
    While, by the twofold grace beguiled
    Of suffering Man and Infant mild,
We walk with Him on faith's calm height
        In vesture white.[3]

[1] in swaddling clothes
[2] in linen for burial
[3] the garment of His righteousness

The Presentation of Jesus in the Temple.

Whiter than snow her infant lay
In Mary's arms that happy day;
    Fairer than all the flowers that blow,
    Brighter than all the stars that glow,
Sky-blossoms in the Milky Way.

Thus I present Him when I pray,
As in the arms of faith, and say,

"Father, there was One Life below
                Whiter than snow!"

That whiteness pleads my cause, I know,
And wins for me the grace to show
    Some reflex rays while here I stray—
    Pledge I shall wear the pure array
In which the Heavenly armies go
                Whiter than snow!

Mary Magdalen at the Cross.

With her clasped hands upraised against the wood
        Stained by His blood,
Beneath the Saviour's piercèd feet she knelt
        And weeping felt
The sprinkled drops from that ensanguined Tree
Where Jesus hung to set the sinner free.

'Mid darkness deep the glory from His face
        Illumed the place,
And showed her anguished eyes uplifted there,
        And golden hair
Which once had wiped the drenching tears away
From His dear feet upon a happier day.

Unutterable love and sorrow now
        Sat on her brow,
As for her sins He gave His precious blood,
        A cleansing flood:
Down from His outstretched hands and thorn-crowned head
The mighty ransom, drop by drop, was shed.

Lord, be it mine beneath Thy cross to kneel,
        And daily feel
The tenderness of gratitude and grief,
        And find relief
From haunting fears that on the conscience rise
In presence of the Glorious Sacrifice.

And when the changing winds of error blow
        Men to and fro,

As ivy clings to the sustaining tree,
    May I to thee
Cling evermore, O Lord, and safe abide,
Clasping in life and death the Crucified!

My Study.

My study! gratefully I gaze around,
    Rejoicing in its quaint and quiet look,
    Each favourite picture and each well-loved book,
And the calm feeling of its sacred ground.
A garden view closed by the narrow bound
    Of buttress'd orchard wall—green, sheltered nook,
    With glimpse of woodland haunted by the rook,[1]
While seen far off the incessant trains resound.
Amidst my books I sit, tranquil, alone,
    And hear afar the great world rushing by,
    My silent work by busy men unnoted:
"Some day," Faith whispers, "'twill be better known,
    Seed sown in secret will bear fruit on high,
    Immortal are the hours to God devoted."

[1] rook—a black, European crow noted for its gregarious habits

Father and Child.

As up and down a shady place
I walked with melancholy pace,
A cloud upon my heart and face
    Of sin and sadness,
Suddenly flashing on the view
My little boy in white and blue
Ran tow'rds me up the avenue
    With look of gladness.

And all a father's love leapt out
Instinctively, and clung about
The child, subduing fear and doubt
    With tender yearning:
As if he had been sent to prove
By living sign that higher Love
Which waits and watches from above
    Each son's returning.

Who made the eye, shall He not see?
The ear, shall He not hear? And He
Who, in creating, gave to me
    A father's feeling,
Shall He not feel?—and kindly greet
A son that weeps before His feet—
With kiss of reconcilement sweet
    His pardon sealing.

For one constraining cause alone
That child was dear—he was my own—
Spontaneously my love had grown—
    And how much rather
Shall I, "the work of His own hand,"
The yearning love of God command—
Can He my prayers and tears withstand
    Who is my Father!

On an Infant's Death.

A little life,
Five summer months of gladness,
Without one cloud of sorrow, sin, or strife—
Cut short by sudden gloom and wintry sadness.

A little mound,
By buttress grey defended,
Watered with tears and garlanded all round,
By gentle hands affectionately tended.

A little cot,
Empty, forlorn, forsaken,
Silent remembrancer that he is not—
Gone—past our voice to lull or kiss or waken.

A little frock
He wore, or hat that shaded
His innocent brow—seen with a sudden shock
Of grief for that dear form so quickly faded.

A little flower,
Because he touched it, cherished—
Fragile memorial of one happy hour
Before the beauty of our blossom perished.

A little hair,
Secured with trembling fingers—
All that is left us of our infant fair,
All we shall see of him while this life lingers.

A little name,
In parish records written,
A passing sigh of sympathy to claim
From other fathers for a father smitten.

But a great trust
Irradiates our sorrow,
That though today his name is writ in dust,
We shall behold it writ in heaven tomorrow.

And a great peace
Our troubled soul possesses,
That though to embrace him these poor arms
    must cease,
Our lamb lies folded in the Lord's caresses.

A little pain
To point his life's brief story—
A few hours' mortal weariness, to gain
Unutterable rest, unending glory.

A little prayer,
By lips Divine once spoken,
"Thy will be done!"—is breathed in the air
From hearts submissive though with accents
    broken.

A little while
And time no more shall sever—
But we shall see him with his own sweet smile,
And clasp our darling in our arms for ever.

Under the Snow.

Our darling of the summer hours,
    Our sunbeam in the summer glow,
Our blossom 'mid the dancing bowers,
        Alas! he lieth low
        Under the snow.

We mourn him through the winter gloom,
    We miss him in the fireside glow,
Which dances round the curtained room,
        The while he lieth low
        Under the snow.

Oh, no! 'tis but our darling's dust;
    He basks in Heaven's eternal glow,
Folded in arms that we can trust:
        He lies not low
        Under the snow.

The Well-Head.

I traced a little brook to its well-head,
    Where, amid quivering weeds, its waters leap
    From the earth, and, hurrying into shadow, creep
Unseen but vocal in their deep-worn bed.
Hawthorns and hazels interlacing wed
    With roses sweet, and overhang the steep
    Moss'd banks, while through the leaves stray sunbeams peep,
And on the whispering stream faint glimmerings shed.
Thus let my life flow on, through green fields gliding,
    Unnoticed not unuseful in its course,

Still fresh and fragrant, though in shadow hiding,
  Holding its destined way with quiet force,
Cheered with the music of a peace abiding,
  Drawn daily from its ever-springing Source.

Fourteen Poems by Richard Wilton (1827–1903)

Richard Wilton was an Anglican pastor whom Frances Ridley Havergal knew and valued. She asked Wilton to help in selecting her own poems for a book Frances was going to publish. He published five volumes of poems. He is very obscure today.

Three Poems by Mary Jane (Deck) Walker

He came, Whose embassy was peace.
  He left His throne above
To prove if enmity would cease
  Beneath the power of love.
He came, Whose errand was to give;
  His hand was opened wide.
Yea, at our need, that we might live,
  He gave Himself—and died.

What had the world for Him? 'twas meet
  To answer love with love,
With signs of thankful joy to greet
  The Stranger from above.
For Him! with all its proud array,
  Of kingdom, palace, tower?
He was a wanderer each day,
  A mourner every hour.

For Him! with all its glory spread
  Before its Maker's sight,
He had not where to lay His head—
  That wearied head, by night.
For Him! His days were almost past,
  His sorrows well-nigh o'er?
But lo, the world will give at last,
  From its abundant store!

The shameful cross, the piercing thorn,
  The vinegar and gall!
The world gives these with cruel scorn,
  And He endures them all.
O world! that cross doth still proclaim,
  On earth—in heaven above,
The story of thy guilt and shame,
  The wonders of His love!

                                        1855.

Jesus, I will trust Thee, trust Thee with my soul;
Guilty, lost, and helpless, Thou canst make me whole.
There is none in heaven or on earth like Thee.
Thou hast died for sinners—therefore, Lord, for me.

Jesus, I may trust Thee, name of matchless worth
Spoken by the angel at Thy wondrous birth;
Written, and for ever, on Thy cross of shame,
Sinners read and worship, trusting in that name.

Jesus, I must trust Thee, pondering Thy ways,
Full of love and mercy all Thine earthly days:
Sinners gathered round Thee, lepers sought Thy face—
None too vile or loathsome for a Saviour's grace.

Jesus, I can trust Thee, trust Thy written word,
Though Thy voice of pity I have never heard.
When Thy Spirit teacheth, to my taste how sweet—
Only may I hearken, sitting at Thy feet.

Jesus, I do trust Thee, trust without a doubt:
"Whosoever cometh, Thou wilt not cast out."
Faithful is Thy promise, precious is Thy blood—
These my soul's salvation, Thou my Saviour God!

1864.

I journey through a desert drear and wild,
Yet is my heart by such sweet thoughts beguiled
Of Him on Whom I lean, my Strength, my Stay,
I can forget the sorrows of the way.

Thoughts of His love—the root of every grace
Which finds in this poor heart a dwelling-place;
The sunshine of my soul, than day more bright,
And my calm pillow of repose by night.

Thoughts of His sojourn in this vale of tears—
The tale of love unfolded in those years
Of sinless suffering and patient grace,
I love again, and yet again, to trace.

Thoughts of His glory—on the cross I gaze,
And there behold its sad yet healing rays;
Beacon of hope, which, lifted up on high,
Illumes with heavenly light the tear-dimmed eye.

Thoughts of His coming, for that joyful day
In patient hope I watch, and wait, and pray.
The dawn draws nigh, the midnight shadows flee;
Oh, what a sunrise will that Advent be!

Thus while I journey on, my Lord to meet,
My thoughts and meditations are so sweet

Of Him on Whom I lean, my Strength, my Stay,
I can forget the sorrows of the way!

1846.

Three Poems by Mary Jane (Deck) Walker (1816–1878)

Eleven Poems by Charlotte Elliott[1]

"Just as I am."

"Him that cometh unto Me I will in no wise cast out." John 6:37

Just as I am—without one plea
But that Thy blood was shed for me,
And that Thou bid'st me come to Thee—
      O Lamb of God, I come!

Just as I am—and waiting not
To rid my soul of one dark blot,
To Thee, whose blood can cleanse each
   spot—
      O Lamb of God, I come!

Just as I am, though toss'd about,
With many a conflict, many a doubt,
Fightings and fears within, without—
      O Lamb of God, I come!

Just as I am—poor, wretched, blind;
Sight, riches, healing of the mind,
Yea, all I need, in Thee I find—
      O Lamb of God, I come!

Just as I am—Thou wilt receive,
Wilt welcome, pardon, cleanse, relieve,
Because Thy promise I believe—
      O Lamb of God, I come!

Just as I am—Thy love unknown
Has broken every barrier down;
Now to be Thine, yea, Thine alone—
      O Lamb of God, I come!

Just as I am—of that free love,
The breadth, length, depth, and height to prove,
Here, for a season, then above—
      O Lamb of God, I come!

On the First Page of a Manuscript Volume.

When to a sinner's hand 'tis given to trace
In this unwritten book the earliest line,
What name, oh! blessed Saviour, should he place
The first upon the virgin leaf but Thine?
So may the savour of that sacred name,
A pledge throughout its future pages be,

[1] Frances Ridley Havergal wrote in a letter in 1869, "I hope you will get to know Charlotte Elliott; it is an honour from God to have had it given her, to write what she has written."

That all unsullied by less hallowed theme,
They ne'er shall bear a trace unworthy Thee.
Fair are they now, like young life's promised days;
Bur ere the leaves are filled and numbered o'er,
Oft shall the glistening eye recall the trace
Of hands that write, and hearts that beat no more.
Oh! then, when many a heart and hand is cold,
Whose fond memento stands recorded here,
May the sweet thought that in Thy book enrolled
Their names are written, chase the rising tear;
But if the tear will fall, the soul will mourn
As memory hangs o'er friendship's severed ties,
Oh! bid it to this page in peace return,
And read Thy name—the Friend that never dies!

The Pilgrim's Want.

I want that adorning Divine,
Thou only, my God, canst bestow;
I want in those beautiful garments to shine,
Which distinguish Thy household below.
Colossians 3:12,17

I want every moment to feel
That Thy Spirit resides in my heart,
That His power is present to cleanse and to heal,
And newness of life to impart.
Romans 8:11,16

I want, oh! I want to attain
Some likeness, my Saviour, to Thee!
That longed-for resemblance once more to regain,
Thy comeliness put upon me!
1 John 3:2,3

I want to be marked for Thine own,
Thy seal on my forehead to wear;
To receive that "new name" on the mystic white stone,
Which none but Thyself can declare.
Revelation 2:17

I want so in Thee to abide,
As to bring forth some fruit to Thy praise!

The branch which Thou prunest, though feeble and dried,
    May languish, but never decays.
            John 15:2,5

I want Thine own hand to unbind
    Each tie to terrestrial things—
Too tenderly cherished, too closely entwined,
    Where my heart too tenaciously clings.
            1 John 2:15

I want, by my aspect serene,
    My actions and words to declare—
That my treasure is placed in a country unseen,
    That my heart's best affections are there.
            Matthew 6:19,21

I want, as a traveller, to haste
    Straight onward, nor pause in my way—
Nor forethought, nor anxious contrivance, to waste
    On the tent only pitched for a day.
            Hebrews 13:5,6

I want—and this sums up my prayer—
    To glorify Thee till I die;
Then calmly to yield up my soul to Thy care,
    And breathe out, in faith, my last sigh.
            Philippians 3:8,9

For the First Leaf of a New Testament.

Saviour, I dwell with ever-new delight
    On all those wondrous lineaments Divine,
    Those matchless words, those God-like acts of Thine,
Which in this book Thy Spirit deigns t'indite.
Oh, purge yet more my intellectual sight,—
    Each sense, each thought, each faculty refine,
    That Thy full radiance on my soul may shine,
While prostrate she implores Thy sacred light;
Then, whether in the lowly manger laid,
    Or in the desert fasting, or withdrawn
    On the cold mount, from eve till dewy morn,
Be my heart and mind on Thee alone stayed;
Thee as Jehovah I shall still adore,
"God over all, blessed for evermore."

On the Funeral Day of a Dear Friend.

"And all wept, and bewailed her: but He said, Weep not; she is not dead, but
sleepeth." Luke 7:52

Yes, lay her in that hallowed bed
Where rested once Immanuel's head,—
But whisper there the words He said,
  "She is not dead, but sleepeth."

Let faith its glorious task perform,
Picturing that now unconscious form
Waking with life and beauty warm—
  "She is not dead, but sleepeth."

Oh! never will she wake again
Sick, weary, feeble, or in pain;
No trace of suffering will remain,
  For she in Jesus sleepeth.

Full many a conflict she has known,
In tears, full often, she has sown;
The fight is fought, the victory won,
  She rests, and sweetly sleepeth.

When the bright beams of glory fill
That narrow chamber dark and still,
She will sit up, and sweetly smile:
  "She is not dead, but sleepeth."

The voice of her Beloved will say,
  "Arise, my fair one, come away!"
Oh with what joy will she obey!
  "She is not dead, but sleepeth."

Then raised in power, in beauty drest,
Jesus will guide the lovely guest,
And place her at the marriage feast:
  "She is not dead, but sleepeth."

In Due Season We Shall Reap If We Faint Not.

My soul, thou art weary within me, and faint;
I hear thee thus breathing thy mournful complaint,
"O when will this harassing warfare be o'er?
O when will mine enemy foil me no more?"

My soul, be not weary—shrink not from the strife;
Redouble thine efforts—it is for thy life—
That soldier alone wears the conqueror's wreath,
Who has proved himself faithful—yea, even to death.

The result is not doubtful, the victory is sure;
But only for those to the end who endure;
And legions invisible, near thee arrayed,
Are watching intently to cheer and to aid.

Nay, more, fainting spirit, look upward and see
Thy Captain omnipotent watching o'er thee;

Giving charge to His angels to keep thee from harm,
Stretching forth for thy succour His sheltering arm.

Look, look unto Him! To the faint He gives power,
Appeal to His love in this suffering hour—
He will look on thee now, as on Gideon of old,
And infuse by that look strength and courage untold.

Be not weary and faint, though the warfare with sin
Must still be continued, without and within—
Be sober, be vigilant, watch to the end—
On the sure word of promise unfaltering depend.

Yes! look unto Jesus, and yield not to fear,
The time of the end is for thee very near;
That Saviour Who chose thee, and made thee His own,
The feeblest He loves will with victory crown.

To Comfort Me.

Jesus! Thou in heaven art pleading
   Even my unworthy cause!
Thou for me art interceding;
   Thy compassion ne'er withdraws.
Canst thou, oh! my soul, repine,
   When so blest a lot is thine?

When my path is dark and dreary,
   And my strength indeed is small;
When my soul is faint and weary,
   Saviour! let me then recall,
Thee, my Advocate above,
   And Thy never-changing love!

For a Dying Bed.

Christ is my hope, Christ is my life,
   Christ is my strength, my victory—
In this dark hour—this final strife,
   Through Christ a conqueror I shall be!
Himself He will beside me stand,
And save me with His own right hand.

Christ is my treasure, Christ my joy,
   I glory in His name alone,
And death each barrier will destroy
   Which keeps me from that glorious
     throne,
Where I shall see Him face to face,
While all His mercies I retrace.

Christ is the Bridegroom of my soul,
   In Him are centered my desires—
Now I have reached the wished-for goal,—
   And my enraptured soul aspires
To dwell with Him (earth's troubles o'er)
For ever, and for evermore!

Arise; this is not your rest.

Alas! how oft I've lingered on my way,
   To raise, in some loved spot, a blissful bower,
   And trained each plant, and cherished every flower,
As I were not "the pilgrim of a day."
Forced by an unseen guardian-hand away,
   How have I spent in tears the bitter hour,
   Because no longer I retained the power
Within my fancied paradise to stay!
But now my hope, my purpose, my desire,
   Is ne'er again on earth to build my nest;
Heavenward in every thought and act to aspire,
   My hourly motto, "This is not your rest!"
And though sweet flowers along my path may bloom,
Still to pass by them, pressing towards my home.

To a Widowed Friend.

"Now no chastening for the present seemeth to be joyous, but grievous; nevertheless afterward it yieldeth the peaceable fruit of righteousness unto them that are exercised thereby. Wherefore lift up the hands which hang down, and the feeble knees." Hebrews 12:11,12

I view thy passage through this vale of tears,
   The sorrows which have marked thy youthful morn,
   And then I grieve thy heart has been so torn
With agitating passions, hopes, and fears.
Oh, may sweet peace attend thy future years,
   Or still may all thy varied griefs be borne
   By Him Whose pity soothes the heart forlorn,
Whose heavenly smile the saddest bosom cheers.
'Tis well for thee the cup of earthly bliss
   So soon was rendered bitter to thy taste;
It was not meant that on a world like this
   Thy heaven-born soul her energies should waste:
Each sorrow whispers, "Seek thy peace above,
And give to God Thy undivided love."

On My Birthday.

There was a wanderer once, who strove in vain
   At earthly fountains to assuage her thirst;
   For though they sparkled and seemed sweet at first,
Soon unabated, it returned again:

But He Who marks and pities human pain,
  And loves to pardon and reclaim the worst,
  Met her, in mercy infinite; as erst
Another wanderer on Samaria's plain.
He led her to the living stream that flows
  From heavenly springs, the pilgrim to restore;
And there she quenched her thirst, and learnt that those
  Who drink that water thirst again no more,
But hasten on, through strength divinely given,
E'en till they reach the fountain-head in heaven.

Eleven Poems by Charlotte Elliott (1789–1871)

O Haupt voll Blut und Wunden.

A Passion Hymn.

O sacred Head! now wounded,
  With grief and shame weighed down,
Now scornfully surrounded
  With thorns, Thine only crown;
O sacred Head! what glory,
  What bliss till now was Thine!
Yet though despised and gory,
  I joy to call Thee mine.

O noblest Brow, and dearest!
  In other days the world
All feared, when Thou appearedst.
  What shame on Thee is hurled!
How art Thou pale with anguish,
  With sore abuse and scorn;
How does that visage languish,
  Which once was bright as morn.

The blushes late residing
  Upon that holy cheek,
The roses once abiding
  Upon those lips so meek,
Alas! they have departed;
  Wan death has rifled all!
For weak and broken-hearted,
  I see Thy body fall.

What Thou, my Lord, hast suffered
  Was all for sinners' gain.
Mine, mine was the transgression,
  But Thine the deadly pain.
Lo! here I fall, my Saviour,
  'Tis I deserve Thy place.
Look on me with Thy favour,
  Vouchsafe to me Thy grace.

Receive me, my Redeemer,
  My Shepherd, make me Thine.
Of every good the fountain,
  Thou art the spring of mine.
Thy lips with love distilling,
  And milk of truth sincere,
With heaven's bliss are filling
  The soul that trembles here.

Beside Thee, Lord, I've taken
  My place—forbid me not!
Hence will I ne'er be shaken,
  Though Thou to death be brought.
If pain's last paleness holds Thee,
  In agony opprest,
Then, then will I enfold Thee
  Within this arm and breast!

The joy can ne'er be spoken
  Above all joys beside,
When in Thy body broken
  I thus with safety hide.
My Lord of life, desiring
  Thy glory now to see,
Beside the cross expiring,
  I'd breathe my soul to Thee.

What language shall I borrow
  To thank Thee dearest Friend,
For this Thy dying sorrow,
  Thy pity without end?
Oh! make me Thine forever,
  And should I fainting be,
Lord, let me never, never
  Outlive my love to Thee.

And when I am departing,
  Oh! part not Thou from me.
When mortal pangs are darting,
  Come, Lord, and set me free.
And when my heart must languish
  Amidst the final throe,
Release me from mine anguish
  By Thine own pain and woe.

Be near me when I'm dying,
  Oh! show Thy cross to me,
And for my succour flying,
  Come, Lord, and set me free.
These eyes, new faith receiving,
  From Jesus shall not move,
For he who dies believing
  Dies safely through Thy love.

A Passion Hymn by Paul Gerhardt (1606–1676)
translated by James Waddell Alexander (1804–1859)

O Haupt voll Blut und Wunden.

Ah wounded Head! Must Thou
Endure such shame and scorn!
The blood is trickling from Thy brow
Pierced by the crown of thorn.
Thou Who wast crown'd on high
With light and majesty,
In deep dishonour here must die,
Yet here I welcome Thee!

Thou noble countenance!
All earthly lights are pale
Before the brightness of that glance,
At which a world shall quail.
How is it quenched and gone!
Those gracious eyes how dim!
Whence grew that cheek so pale and wan?
Who dared to scoff at Him?

All lovely hues of life,
That glow'd on lip and cheek,
Have vanish'd in that awful strife;
The Mighty One is weak.
Pale death has won the day,
He triumphs in this hour
When Strength and Beauty fade away,
And yield them to his power.

Ah Lord, Thy woes belong,
Thy cruel pains, to me,
The burden of my sin and wrong
Hath all been laid on Thee.
Behold me where I kneel,
Wrath were my rightful lot,
One glance of love yet let me feel!
Redeemer, spurn me not!

My Guardian, own me Thine;
My Shepherd, bear me home:
O Fount of mercy, Source Divine,
From Thee what blesssings come!
How oft Thy mouth has fed
My soul with angels' food,
How oft Thy Spirit o'er me shed
His stores of heavenly good!

Ah would that I could share
Thy cross, Thy bitter woes!
All true delight lies hidden there,
Thence all true comfort flows.
Ah well were it for me
That I could end my strife,
And die upon the cross with Thee,
Who art my Life of life!

My soul is all o'erfraught,
O Jesus, dearest Friend,
With thankful love to Him Who sought
Such woe for such an end.
Grant me as true a faith,
As Thou art true to me,
That so the icy sleep of death
Be but a rest in Thee.

Yes, when I must depart,
Depart Thou not from me;
When Death is creeping to my heart,
Bear Thou mine agony.
When faith and courage sink,
O'erwhelm'd with dread dismay,
Come Thou Who ne'er from pain didst shrink,
And chase my fears away.

Come to me ere I die,
My comfort and my shield;
Then gazing on Thy cross can I
Calmly my spirit yield.
On Thee, when life is past,
My darkening eyes shall dwell,
My heart in faith shall hold Thee fast;
Who dieth thus, dies well.

Paul Gerhardt. 1659.
translated by Catherine Winkworth (1827–1878)

Six Poems by Horatius Bonar

Our Battle.

How goes the fight with thee,—
The life-long battle with all evil things?
Thine no low strife, and thine no selfish aim;
It is the war of giants and of kings.

Goes the fight well with thee,—
This living fight with death and death's dark power?

Is not the stronger than the strong one near,
    With thee and for thee in the fiercest hour?

Does it grow slacker now?
    Then tremble; for be sure thy hellish foe
Slacks not. 'Tis thou that slackest in the fight.'
    Fainter and feebler falls each weary blow.

Dread not the din and smoke,
    The stifling poison of the fiery air;
Courage! it is the battle of thy God;
    Go, and for Him learn how to do and dare!

What though ten thousand fall,
    And the red field with the dear dead be strewn!
Grasp but more bravely thy bright shield and sword;
    Fight to the last, although thou fight'st alone.

What though ten thousand faint,
    Desert, or yield, or in weak terror flee?
Heed not the panic of the multitude;
    Thine be the Captain's watchword—Victory!

Look to thine armour well!
    Thine the one panoply no blow that fears;
Ours is the day of rusted swords and shields,
    Of loosened helmets and of broken spears.

Heed not the throng of foes!
    To fight 'gainst hosts is still the Church's lot.
Side thou with God, and thou must win the day;
    Woe to the man 'gainst whom hell fighteth not!

Say not the fight is long:
    'Tis but one battle and the fight is o'er;
No second warfare mars thy victory,
    And the one triumph is for evermore.

I hear the words of love.

I hear the words of love,
    I gaze upon the blood,
I see the mighty Sacrifice,
    And I have peace with God.

'Tis everlasting peace!
    Sure as Jehovah's name;
'Tis stable as His steadfast throne,
    For evermore the same.

The clouds may go and come,
  And storms may sweep my sky—
The blood-sealed friendship changes not;
  The cross is ever nigh.

My love is ofttimes low,
  My joy still ebbs and flows;
But peace with Him remains the same,
  No change Jehovah knows.

I change, He changes not,
  The Christ can never die;
His love, not mine, the resting place,
His truth, not mine, the tie.

"Come unto Me, all ye that labour."

Matthew 11:28

I heard the voice of Jesus say,
  "Come unto Me and rest:
Lay down, thou weary one, lay down
  Thy head upon My breast."
I came to Jesus as I was—
  Weary, and worn, and sad;
I found in Him a resting place,
  And He has made me glad.

I heard the voice of Jesus say,
  "Behold, I freely give
The living water; thirsty one,
  Stoop down and drink, and live."
I came to Jesus and I drank
  Of that life-giving stream;
My thirst was quenched, my soul revived,
  And now I live in Him.

I heard the voice of Jesus say,
  "I am this dark world's Light;
Look unto Me, thy morn shall rise,
  And all thy day be bright."
I looked to Jesus and I found
  In Him my Star, my Sun;
And in that light of life I'll walk,
  Till travelling days are done.

"The Lord hath laid on Him the iniquity of us all."

Isaiah 53:6

I lay my sins on Jesus,
  The spotless Lamb of God;
He bears them all and frees us
  From the accursed load.
I bring my guilt to Jesus,
  To wash my crimson stains
White in His blood most precious,
  Till not a spot remains.

I lay my wants on Jesus;
  All fulness dwells in Him;
He heals all my diseases,
  He doth my soul redeem.
I lay my griefs on Jesus,
  My burdens and my cares:
He from them all releases,
  He all my sorrows shares.

I rest my soul on Jesus,
    This weary soul of mine:
His right hand me embraces,
    I on His breast recline.
I love the name of Jesus,
    Immanuel, Christ, the Lord;
Like fragrance on the breezes,
    His name abroad is poured.

I long to be like Jesus,
    Meek, loving, lowly, mild;
I long to be like Jesus,
    The Father's holy child;
I long to be with Jesus,
    Amid the heavenly throng,
To sing with saints His praises,
    To learn the angels' song.

"Now returned unto the Shepherd."

I Peter 2:25

I was a wand'ring sheep,
    I did not love the fold;
I did not love my Shepherd's voice,
    I would not be controll'd.
I was a wayward child,
    I did not love my home;
I did not love my Father's voice,
    I lov'd afar to roam.

They spoke in tender love,
    They rais'd my drooping head;
They gently clos'd my bleeding wounds,
    My fainting soul they fed.
They wash'd my guilt away,
    They made me clean and fair;
They brought me to my home in peace—
    The long-sought wanderer!

The Shepherd sought His sheep,
    The Father sought His child;
They follow'd me o'er vale and hill,
    O'er deserts waste and wild:
They found me nigh to death,
    Famish'd, and faint, and lone;
They bound me with the bands of love;
    They sav'd the wand'ring one!

Jesus my Shepherd is,
    'Twas He that lov'd my soul,
'Twas He that wash'd me in His blood,
    'Twas He that made me whole.
'Twas He that sought the lost,
    That found the wand'ring sheep,
'Twas He that brought me to the fold,
    'Tis He that still doth keep.

I was a wand'ring sheep,
    I would not be controll'd;
But now I love the Shepherd's voice,
    I love, I love, the fold!
I was a wayward child,
    I once preferr'd to roam;
But now I love my Father's voice,
    I love, I love His home!

Thy way, not mine, O Lord.

Psalm 107:7 "He led them by the right way."

Thy way, not mine, O Lord,
   However dark it be!
Lead me by Thine own hand,
   Choose Thou the path for me.

Smooth let it be or rough,
   It will be still the best;
Winding or straight, it leads
   Right onward to Thy rest.

I dare not choose my lot;
   I would not, if I might;
Choose Thou for me, my God;
   So shall I walk aright.

The kingdom that I seek
   Is Thine; so let the way
That leads to it be Thine;
   Else I must surely stray.

Take Thou my cup, and it
   With joy or sorrow fill,
As best to Thee may seem;
   Choose Thou my good or ill.

Choose Thou for me my friends,
   My sickness or my health;
Choose Thou my cares for me,
   My poverty or wealth.

Not mine—not mine the choice,
   In things or great or small;
Be Thou my Guide, my Strength,
   My Wisdom and my All!

Six Poems by Horatius Bonar (1808–1889)

Proverbs 24:11-12

11 הַצֵּל לְקֻחִים לַמָּוֶת וּמָטִים לַהֶרֶג אִם־תַּחְשֹׂוךְ:
12 כִּי־תֹאמַר הֵן לֹא־יָדַעְנוּ זֶה הֲלֹא־תֹכֵן לִבּוֹת הוּא־יָבִין
וְנֹצֵר נַפְשְׁךָ הוּא יֵדָע וְהֵשִׁיב לְאָדָם כְּפָעֳלוֹ:

Proverbs 24:11,12 "If thou forbear to deliver them that are drawn unto death, and those that are ready to be slain; if thou sayest, Behold, we knew it not: doth not He that pondereth the heart consider it? and He that keepeth thy soul, doth not He know it? and shall not He render to every man according to his works?"

A World Gone Mad.

I see them come to my home
With loud knocks at my door;
Then I open to hatred,
It's no use to implore.

My wife's face shows her fright,
How I ache for my child;
I try to comfort,
So I force a brave smile.

Streets seem so deserted,
And our friends now so few;
They turn their backs on us,
Just because we are Jews.

My child cries, "Daddy,
Please don't leave me alone;"
So I hug her and kiss her,
Then she's gone—and I groan.

I see them walk slowly,
Then they're forced on a train;
Now I'm packed in like cattle,
Will I see them again?

That hated yellow star,
We Jews are forced to wear,
And a twisted Nazi cross,
Does anybody care?

There's Auschwitz, Bergen-Belsen,
Dachau—to name a few;
Those hell-holes that are whispered,
As death camps for a Jew.

I see chimneys smoking,
What is that awful smell?
If we Jews are placed in there,
This world has turned to hell.

Where are the Christian voices?
Where is the statesman's shout?
I thought the love of neighbor,
Was what it's all about.

Why do I hear but curses,
As if I'm something bad;
And as a Jew, die all alone,
In a world that's gone mad.

Dr. Frank Eiklor, Shalom International

Matthew 22:37–40 "Jesus said unto him, Thou shalt love the Lord thy God with all thy heart, and with all thy soul, and with all thy mind. This is the first and great commandment. And the second is like unto it, Thou shalt love thy neighbour as thyself. On these two commandments hang all the law and the prophets."

The Refiner's Fire.

He sat by a furnace of sevenfold heat,
  As He watched by the precious ore,
And closer He bent with a searching gaze
  As He heated it more and more.
He knew He had ore that could stand the test,
  And He wanted the finest gold,
To mold as a crown, for the King to wear,
  Set with gems of price untold.
So He laid our gold in the burning fire,
  Tho' we fain would say Him, "Nay";
And watched the dross that we had not seen,
  As it melted and passed away.
And the gold grew brighter and yet more bright,
  But our eyes were dim with tears,

We saw but the fire—not the Master's hand,
   And questioned with anxious fears.
Yet our gold shone out with a richer glow
   As it mirrored a Form above,
That bent o'er the fire, tho' unseen by us,
   With a look of ineffable love.
Can we think it pleases His loving heart
   To cause us a moment's pain?
Ah, no! but He sees through the present cross
   The bliss of eternal gain.
So He waited there with a watchful eye,
   With a love that is strong and sure,
And His gold did not suffer a bit more heat
   Than was needed to make it pure.

Author unknown.

Luke 7:36-50.

Forgiven, redeemed, full of love she came
   to express her love to Him Who is love,
     Who so loved that He came here from above:
God in flesh, to show God's truth, heal sick, blind, lame,
give Himself for sinners. He said her fame
   would be told where e'er His truth is preached. Love
     filled her—was all of her—to Christ. Sweet Dove,
so fill my heart with love to Him the same.
Lord Jesus Christ, this is my heart's desire:
   to love Thee so, to worship at Thy feet.
Love, thanks, praise, worship, like a fervent fire
   keep burning in me, consuming complete
my all to Thee. Lord, her love came from Thee.
Truth of God, Love of God, do so to me.

David Chalkley April 20, 1999

Four Hymns by William E. Payne

Beneath the sky of Judah's night,	The angels o'er the manger bend;
Beneath the special star so bright,	They vainly try to comprehend,
The wonder of the ages see,	Within the borrowed cradle stall,
A Saviour born for you and me.	A new born babe, but Lord of all.

The shepherds come, the wise men too;
They gaze in wonder at the view.
The heavenly hosts rejoice to sing,
And draw attention to their King.

Let Christian voices join the praise,
And celebrate this day of days.
Let God be worshipped and adored,
For this great gift of Christ the Lord.

The promised Lord has come,
    Foretold through many years;
The theme of angels' song
    At last on earth appears.

What miracle is this!
    Greater than words can tell,
That in a maiden's arms
    Should lie Emmanuel.

Born in a stable bare,
    And in a manger laid,
The sovereign Lord of all
    Who heaven and earth has made.

The angels speak of Him,
    "A Saviour, Christ, the Lord";
Incarnate Son of God
    By all of heaven adored.

Then let us too adore.
    'Twas for our sakes He came.
Through all our earthly life
    Let us exalt His name.

Bread and wine, what simple emblems,
    But of love divine they speak,
And declare a gracious Saviour,
    Who came down the lost to seek.

Solemn moments, oh how precious,
    In remembrance now we bow;
Here by faith we see His sorrows,
    And renew to Him our vow.

As we gather at the table,
    Hearts are drawn to Calvary's tree,
And we hear again His whisper,
    "Sinner, I bore all for thee."

Here again we are reminded
    Of the path the Saviour trod,
So that we, though vile and sinful,
    Might be reconciled to God.

Thus together we adore Him,
    Him Who for us bled and died.
May to Him all praise be given,
    Jesus Christ the Crucified.

Salvation all of sovereign grace,
    Well may our hearts rejoice,
To think that sinners such as we
    Were objects of God's choice;
That love divine was set on us
    Before the world began,
And all the details of our life
    Included in God's plan.

Salvation all of sovereign grace,
    Well may our praise abound;
In Christ the dead are made to live,
    By Him the lost are found.
He has redeemed us by His blood;
    He has our sins forgiven.
He's set our feet upon the road
    That leads us on to heaven.

Salvation all of sovereign grace,
Then give to God the praise;
For He Who has begun the work
Maintains it all our days.
Preserving grace He will bestow
That we might faithful be;
He saves not just for time alone,
But for eternity.

Four Hymns by William E. Payne (1936–1997)

Grace Sufficient.

2 Corinthians 12:9.

When all seems lost,
And too great the cost;
When no light in the darkness I see:
Then the Lord speaks clear
Through the shadow drear:
"My grace is sufficient for thee."

When call to prayer
Sees no answer there,
Yet united in prayer all agree;
Still the Lord knows best.
On His Word I rest:
"My grace is sufficient for thee."

The path winds long,
And no joyful song
Lifts the soul's mournful, muted key.
Then I hear Him say
On the upward way,
"My grace is sufficient for thee."

Loved ones depart,
Leaving aching heart:
Answer sought in humble plea.
His Word, ever true,
Now reaches to you,
"My grace is sufficient for thee."

All that I need
Is His Word indeed,
Day by day to eternity.
Just take I His hand,
On His Word I stand:
Thy cross is sufficient for me.

Stanley F. Ward

Seven Hymns by Christopher Idle

Isaiah 53.

Who believes what we have heard,
who has seen God's power made known?
when the Servant of the Lord
grew unnoticed and alone:

undesired by those around
and unlovely in their eyes,
like a root in desert ground
which men trample and despise.

Yet for us the Servant grieved,
all our sorrows he endured;
his the torment unrelieved,
his the bruising from the Lord.
here is all our guilt engraved,
here are all our wrongs revealed;
by his suffering we are saved,
by his tortures we are healed.

Far away like sheep we strayed,
by our own desires misled,
but the Lord our God has laid
all our sins upon his head.
to the slaughter once he came—
see the willing victim stand
as a sacrificial lamb
silent at the killer's hand.

So he spent his final breath,
all his life for us he gave;
men of violence shared his death,
and a rich man lent his grave.
target of his people's hate,
by oppression snatched away—
who was mindful of his fate,
who considered it that day?

But he now prolongs his days,
raised from darkness into light;
sees his children bring their praise,
vindicates and sets them right.
for the criminals he prayed,
for their crimes he bled and died;
now the sacrifice is made,
and the Servant satisfied.

Matthew 5:1,2; 7:28,29.

Teach me, Lord Jesus, all I need to know:
    form within me your mind;
    let all the truth I find
make me more humble, more truly to grow.

Teach me, Lord Jesus, all I need to do:
    help me by love to live,
    suffer and work and give,
learning obedience, and learning from you.

Teach me, Lord Jesus, all I need to say:
    set my tongue free to speak
    true words, and pure and meek,
patterned on yours, which shall not pass away.

Teach me, Lord Jesus, all I need to be:
    train me and put me right
    till I reflect your light,
till you complete all your purpose for me.

Acts 17:24-29.

Lord, you need no house,
no manger now, nor tomb;
yet come, I pray, to make
my heart your home.

Lord, you need no gift,
for all things come from you;
receive what you have given—
my heart renew.

Lord, you need no skill
to make your likeness known;
create your image here—
my heart your throne.

Romans 10:9-11.

Make us, O God, ashamed of sin,
and give its power no place;
but not ashamed that we have been
adopted by your grace.

Ashamed of all our loveless words
which hurt or wound or maim,
but not ashamed to be the Lord's
and speak your holy name.

Make us ashamed of every flaw
in hearts which you lay bare;
but not ashamed, if your pure law
is clearly written there.

Make us ashamed to use our hands
as selfish tools of greed;
but not ashamed of your commands
to serve our neighbour's need.

So when our God is fully known
and all his power acclaimed,
when heaven and earth and hell bow down,
we shall not be ashamed.

2 Corinthians 4:4.

I never looked for Jesus;
praise God, he looked for me!
By the blinding sin that held me in
I could never truly see.

I spent no love on Jesus;
he spent his blood for me:
for the source of love is God above,
and it meant his agony.

I paid no heed to Jesus;
he paid in full for me.
To release a slave his life he gave,
and he bought my liberty.

I had no time for Jesus;
he made the time for me:
and he shows me how to serve him
and enjoy eternity.   [now

I have no claims on Jesus
but he has claims on me;
and his greatest claim is still the same
as it was on Calvary.

Hebrews 4:12,13.

How sure the Scriptures are!
God's vital, urgent word,
as true as steel, and far
more sharp than any sword.
    So deep and fine
    at his control
    they pierce where soul
    and spirit join.

They test each human thought,
refining like a fire;
they measure what we ought
to do and to desire.
    For God knows all;
    exposed it lies
    before his eyes
    to whom we call.

Let those who hear his voice
confronting them today
reject the tempting choice
of doubting or delay.
    For God speaks still;
    his word is clear,
    so let us hear
    and do his will.

As the Light upon the River.

As the light upon the river
at the rising of the sun,
shine, O Lord, upon our city;
here on earth your will be done.
here we meet in glad thanksgiving,
worship, praise, and prayer we bring,
grief for sin and joy for mercy—
all for you, O Christ our King.

Crucified and risen Saviour,
God incarnate, First and Last,
yours the city of the future,
yours the pilgrims of the past:
Lord, revive your weary people!
Let your voice again be heard;
rid your church of all excuses
for our deafness to your word.

From our failure and our blindness,
bound by debts we cannot pay,
God of Jubilee, release us—
O renew us all, we pray!
In a world exhausted, restless,
still oppressing and oppressed,
Lord of Sabbath, bring us freedom,
resurrection, life, and rest.

Strengthen us to love our neighbours—
welcome strangers at our door,
find the lost and reach the lonely
so that they shall weep no more:
in our homes, our crowded journeys,
work or leisure, calm or noise,
come to satisfy our longings,
Christ the Joy of all our joys!

As the rain upon the garden,
as the water from the spring,
pour on us your Holy Spirit,
gifts to use and songs to sing:
as the light upon the river
at the rising of the sun,
shine, O Lord, upon our city—
as in heaven, your will be done.

Seven Hymns by Christopher Idle

Two Hymns by John Ryland

Sovereign Ruler of the skies,
Ever gracious, ever wise;
All my times are in Thy hand,
All events at Thy command.

He that formed me in the womb,
He shall guide me to the tomb;
All my times shall ever be
Ordered by His wise decree.

His decrees Who formed the earth,
Fixed my first and second birth;
Parents, native place, and time,
All appointed were by Him.

Times the tempter's power to prove,
Times to taste the Saviour's love;
All must come, and last, and end,
As shall please my heavenly Friend.

Plagues and deaths around me fly;
Till He bids I cannot die;
Not a single shaft can hit
Till the God of love sees fit.

O Lord, we would delight in Thee,
    And on Thy care depend;
To Thee in every trouble flee,
    Our safe, unfailing Friend.

When human cisterns all are dried,
    Thy fulness is the same;
May we with this be satisfied,
    And glory in Thy name.

Why should we thirst for ought below,
    While there's a fountain near,
A fountain which doth ever flow
    The fainting heart to cheer?

No good in creatures can be found;
    All, all is found in Thee:
We must have all things and abound
    Through Thy sufficiency.

Thou that hast made our heaven secure
    Wilt here all good provide;
While Thou art rich, can we be poor—
    Thou who for us hast died?

O Lord, we cast each care on Thee,
    And triumph and adore;
O that our great concern may be
    To love and praise Thee more.

Two Hymns by John Ryland (1753–1825)

Lord, make of me Thine instrument
    Solely to show forth Thy praise.
Play upon me as I cannot
    Music of Thy truth and grace.   David Chalkley

God in His wisdom has ordained and created the temporal and the eternal, and has
knitted them together – the temporal as His way and means to the eternal and Himself.
In His love He took on flesh and blood and bones just like us, to bring us to Himself.

Six Hymns by Dr. Alan Clifford

The Omnipotent Grace of God (Romans 5-8).

Dedicated to the Huguenots and the Lord's persecuted people of every age and generation.

Almighty Father, Lord and King,
Your suffering saints unite to sing
    With holy jubilation!
We worship now before your throne,
Rejoicing since we are your own
    By merciful adoption;
Presdestined to behold your face,
Chosen to know such matchless grace,
    Our souls rejoice with trembling;
Confiding in your sovereign power,
We are secure from hour to hour,
    For God, our God, is reigning!

Almighty Saviour, Son divine
In whom the Father's glories shine,
    Accept our adoration;
Holy Redeemer, you have died,
We by your blood are justified,
    Freed from all condemnation!
Jesus, our Prophet, Priest, and King,
Your ransomed ones rejoice to sing,
    Despite our tribulation;
We conquer through your mighty love,
We have the victory from above,
    Blest by your intercession.

Almighty Spirit, by your breath
All God's elect are raised from death;
   Blessèd regeneration!
Spirit of Christ, come reign within,
Subdue we pray, our every sin,
   Receive our supplication;
Help us in our infirmity,
Strengthen the sons of liberty;
   In earnest expectation,
May we with joy, and patiently,
Wait for the glory yet to be,
   Assured of our redemption!

Grace Triumphant (Isaiah 64; Romans 3:10-26).

Come our God, display your glory,
   Let mankind your power know,
Not in judgement but in mercy,
   Rend the heavens, your grace bestow:
     Let your word,
     Now be heard,
Make your gracious conquest, Lord!

Sin abounds with great dominion,
   Human hearts are all enslaved,
Grant your creatures, Lord, redemption,
   Now may guilty souls be saved!
     May our race,
     Through your grace,
View your love in Jesu's face.

May the song of sins forgiven
   Echo over all the earth,
Angels, with the saints in heaven,
   Join to celebrate new birth:
     We rejoice
     With one voice,
Praising you, our happy choice!

Soon the work of our salvation,
   Once begun, shall be complete,
All your church, brought to perfection,
   Then shall worship at your feet:
     We shall raise
     Hymns of praise,
Through the bliss of endless days!

In Sickness or Distress (II Corinthians 12:9).

Incarnate God, my heavenly friend,
Infinite love which knows no end,
My weakness Thou hast stooped to share,
To taste and feel my every care.

When body, heart, and mind are weak,
So feeble that I cannot speak,
Yet in my most lethargic hour
I rest, my God, upon Thy power.

When human company is near,
My heart can still consume with fear;
But when Lord Jesus, Thou dost call,
My faith then triumphs over all!

Stay by me, Lord Immanuel,
Thy presence, who the joy can tell?
When in distress I sense Thee near,
My eye can shed a joyful tear.

When bitter thoughts and doubts arise,
Let me direct my longing eyes
And fix my gaze upon Thy throne,
Content to know I am Thine own.

When I am weak, then am I strong,
My Saviour then is all my song!
Almighty grace comes to my aid
From Him who heaven and earth has made.

Throughout earth's weary wilderness,
My trusting heart will ever bless
The comforts of redeeming grace,
Which shine from my Immanuel's face.

When I approach life's final hour,
Lord Jesus, be Thy love my power;
In pain or peace, be at my side
And keep me, who for me hast died!

The Beatitudes (Matthew 5:1-12).

Happy are those who yearn for God,
    Who feel their need of grace;
They humbly wait to hear His word,
    To see their Saviour's face.

Happy are those who mourn for sin,
    Their sadness shall depart;
The Spirit's calm shall dwell within,
    His comfort fill the heart.

Happy are those whose hearts are meek,
    Their sins are all forgiven;
They shall inherit all they seek,
    The earth renewed – and heaven.

Happy are those who long to know
    The righteousness divine;
For this they hunger here below
    Till pure in heaven they shine.

Happy are those who mercy show,
    When men would vengeance cry;
Their constant, daily need they know,
    And God has rich supply.

Happy are those whose hearts are pure,
    They have a single eye;
Their one expectant hope is sure,
    To see their God on high.

Happy are those who bring God's peace
    To lives disturbed by sin;
They best can make all conflict cease
    Who know that peace within.

Happy are those who suffer shame
    For Jesus and His word;
They triumph in His saving name,
    And sure is their reward.

Psalm 27.

Lord of my life, my strength, my light,
    O God of my salvation;
I need not fear my enemy's might,
    For sure is my protection.

One thing have I desired of Thee,
    My all-consuming passion!
To dwell with Thee, Thy beauty see,
    The beatific vision!

In times of trouble and dismay,
    Thou art my consolation;
With confidence to Thee I pray,
    My rock, my sure foundation.

To Thee, my God, my praise I bring,
    My foes are in confusion!
I offer Thee, victorious King,
    My poor heart's adoration.

Throughout my life, Thee will I seek;
 Save me from desolation;
Forsake me not, help of the weak,
 My God, my sure salvation.

Make plain my path, teach me Thy way,
 O give me Thy direction;
In life's dark night, be Thou my day,
 My joy and benediction.

I rest upon Thy promise, Lord,
 Strengthen my resolution;
Whilst here below, I trust Thy word,
 Waiting for my redemption.

A Felt Salvation (Romans 14:17).

My dear Redeemer and my God,
 Your glory will I sing!
The Father's image, living Word,
 I worship You, my King.

What truths You have displayed to me!
 What precious words I read;
What depths in Scripture now I see,
 What promises to plead!

My heart Your dying love has won,
 From guilt my soul is free!
My living Lord, Your reign within
 Secures my liberty.

Your grace has now my heart subdued,
 I bow before Your throne;
Your Spirit has my soul renewed,
 Jesus, I'm all Your own!

Your gracious reign, O King divine,
 Begun, shall never cease,
For righteousness and joy are mine,
 And heaven's eternal peace.

Six Hymns by Dr. Alan Clifford

Only Jesus Christ alone can do His truth in a person.

The only true source, and the only true goal and end, of holiness is "Jesus only, Jesus ever, Jesus all in all."

Trouble and need are means of God to bring us to Himself.

The Lord Jesus Christ does what He says, and He finishes what He begins.
Revelation 3:14 Revelation 19:11 Philippians 1:6 Colossians 2:10

Every good gift is the Lord's creation, truly reflective of Him, and all His gifts are given to point us to Himself, and He is Himself His own best gift.

God has so very richly and compassionately communicated to us by His Word: the Word made flesh, God's own and only Son, the Lord Jesus Christ, the faithful and true witness, and the written Word, the Scriptures, His own and very words to us.

After F.R.H.'s poem "Love for Love" (also called "Stay and Think") on pages 281–282 of Volume I: There is no motivation like love. The love of God in His Son, the Lord Jesus Christ, His indescribable love in "even the death of the cross." To know the love of Christ to sinners leaves one heartfully wanting to obey, love, please Him alone.

Mark 10:18 "And Jesus said unto him, Why callest thou me good? There is none good but one, that is, God."
Truth, Lord. Thou art good, for Thou art God.

"I wish, my brothers and sisters, that during this year you may live nearer to Christ than you have ever done before. Depend upon it, it is when we think much of Christ that we think little of ourselves, little of our troubles, and little of the doubts and fears that surround us. Begin from this day, and may God help you. Never let a single day pass over your head without a visit to the garden of Gethsemane, and the cross on Calvary. And as for some of you who are not saved, and know not the Redeemer, I would to God that this very day you would come to Christ."
     Charles Haddon Spurgeon, in a Sermon preached on Sunday morning,
     January 1, 1860, at Exeter Hall, Strand

Deus veritatem amat, et suus Filius solus Jesus Christus veritas est, et Deum amans veritatem amat.
God loves the truth, and His only Son Jesus Christ is the truth, and the one who loves God loves the truth.

"Think much on the love of Jesus Christ." Adoniram Judson

Philippians 4:8 "Finally, brethren, whatsoever things are true, whatsoever things are honest, whatsoever things are just, whatsoever things are pure, whatsoever things are lovely, whatsoever things are of good report, if there be any virtue and if there be any praise, think on these things."

Jesus Christ is true, honest, just, pure, lovely. Of Him there is good report: of Him the Father said, "This is My beloved Son, in Whom I am well pleased. Hear Him." In Him alone is true virtue, and to Him alone belongs true praise.

Isaiah 26:3,4 "Thou wilt keep him in perfect peace, whose mind is stayed on Thee, because he trusteth in Thee. Trust ye in the Lord forever, for in the Lord Jehovah is everlasting strength."

Eight Poems by Frances Ridley Havergal

Without Christ.

"At that time ye were without Christ."—Ephesians 2:12.

John 6:68	I could not do without Thee,
Luke 19:10	O Saviour of the lost!
I Peter 1:18,19	Whose precious blood redeemed me,
Revelation 5:9	At such tremendous cost.
Romans 3:22	Thy righteousness, Thy pardon,
Ephesians 1:7	Thy precious blood must be
Hebrews 6:19	My only hope and comfort,
Galatians 6:14	My glory and my plea!
Psalm 73:23	I could not do without Him!
Song of Solomon 5:10	Jesus is more to me
Philippians 3:8	Than all the richest, fairest gifts
Matthew 13:44	Of earth could ever be.
I Peter 2:7	But the more I find Him precious,
Psalm 18:2	And the more I find Him true,
Psalm 34:8	The more I long for you to find
John 1:46	What He can be to you.
Hosea 13:9	You need not do without Him,
Matthew 20:30	For He is passing by;
Isaiah 30:18	He is waiting to be gracious,
Isaiah 30:19	Only waiting for your cry.
II Corinthians 6:17	He is waiting to receive you,—
Isaiah 43:1	To make you all His own!
Hosea 11:8	Why will you do without Him,
Hosea 14:2	And wander on alone?
Hosea 13:10	Why will you do without Him?
Titus 3:4	Is He not kind indeed?
Romans 5:8	Did He not die to save you?
John 4:14	Is He not all you need?
Acts 5:31	Do you not want a Saviour?
John 15:14	Do you not want a Friend?
Hosea 2:20	One who will love you faithfully,
John 13:1	And love you to the end?

Jeremiah 4:30	Why will you do without Him?
Matthew 24:35	The Word of God is true;
I John 2:17	The world is passing to its doom,
Psalm 144:4	And you are passing too.
James 4:14	It may be, no to-morrow
Proverbs 27:1	Shall dawn for you or me;
Proverbs 29:1	Why will you run the awful risk
Isaiah 33:14	Of all eternity?

Hosea 9:5	What will you do without Him
Ecclesiastes 12:1	In the long and dreary day
Isaiah 59:9,10	Of trouble and perplexity,
Hosea 2:6	When you do not know the way;
Hosea 13:9,10	And no one else can help you,
Jeremiah 2:17	And no one guides you right,
Jeremiah 2:25	And hope comes not with morning,
Job 7:4	And rest comes not with night?

Romans 7:24	You could not do without Him,
John 8:33,34	If once He made you see
II Peter 2:19	The fetters that enchain you
Romans 8:2	Till He hath set you free;
Psalm 38:4	If once you saw the fearful load
Ezekiel 33:10	Of sin upon your soul,—
Jeremiah 17:9	The hidden plague that ends in death,
Jeremiah 17:14	Unless He makes you whole!

Jeremiah 12:5	What will you do without Him
Ecclesiastes 12:3	When death is drawing near,
Song of Solomon 8:6,7	Without His love—the only love
I John 4:18	That casts out every fear;
Jeremiah 13:16	When the shadow-valley opens,
Job 8:13,14	Unlighted and unknown,
Job 10:21,22	And the terrors of its darkness
Psalm 23:4	Must all be passed alone?

Revelation 6:17	What will you do without Him
Revelation 20:11	When the great White Throne is set,
Romans 2:16	And the Judge who never can mistake,
Hosea 7:2	And never can forget,—
II Corinthians 5:10	The Judge, whom you have never here
Matthew 7:23	As Friend and Saviour sought,

| Romans 14:12 | Shall summon you to give account |
| Matthew 12:36 | Of deed, and word, and thought? |

Matthew 25:11	What will you do without Him
Revelation 3:7	When He hath shut the door,
Hebrews 3:19	And you are left outside, because
John 5:40	You would not come before;
Luke 13:25	When it is no use knocking,
Hebrews 12:17	No use to stand and wait,
Revelation 22:11	For the word of doom tolls through your heart,
Luke 16:26	That terrible "Too late"?

John 14:6	You cannot do without Him!
I Timothy 2:5	There is no other name
Acts 4:12	By which you ever can be saved,—
Ephesians 2:12	No way, no hope, no claim!
Mark 8:36	Without Him—everlasting loss
John 3:36	Of love, and life, and light!
Matthew 25:41	Without Him—everlasting woe,
Matthew 8:12	And everlasting night.

Song of Solomon 4:8	But with Him—oh ! with Jesus!—
John 17:24	Are any words so blest?
Isaiah 35:10	With Jesus—everlasting joy
I Thessalonians 4:17	And everlasting rest!
Psalm 107:9	With Jesus—all the empty heart
Ephesians 3:19,20	Filled with His perfect love!
Isaiah 26:3	With Jesus—perfect peace below,
Psalm 16:11	And perfect bliss above!

Jeremiah 5:31	Why should you do without Him?—
Revelation 3:20	It is not yet too late;
II Corinthians 6:2	He has not closed the day of grace,
Matthew 7:13	He has not shut the gate.
Mark 10:49	He calls you!—hush!
John 6:67	He calls you!—He would not have you go
Hosea 2:14	Another step without Him,
John 15:13	Because He loves you so.

Ezekiel 33:11	Why will you do without Him?
John 7:37	He calls and calls again—
Matthew 11:28	"Come unto Me! Come unto Me!"
Isaiah 65:1,2	Oh, shall He call in vain?

Matthew 23:37	He wants to have you with Him;
Psalm 13:1,2	Do you not want Him too?
I John 5:12	You cannot do without Him,
Jeremiah 31:3	And He wants—even you!

"By Thy Cross and Passion."

"He hath given us rest by His sorrow, and life by His death."—John Bunyan.

What hast Thou done for me, O mighty Friend,
    Who lovest to the end !
Reveal Thyself, that I may now behold
    Thy love unknown, untold,
Bearing the curse, and made a curse for me,
That blessed and made a blessing I might be.

Oh, Thou wast crowned with thorns, that I might wear
    A crown of glory fair;
"Exceeding sorrowful," that I might be
    Exceeding glad in Thee;
"Rejected and despised," that I might stand
Accepted and complete on Thy right hand.

Wounded for my transgression, stricken sore,
    That I might 'sin no more';
Weak, that I might be always strong in Thee;
    Bound, that I might be free;
Acquaint with grief, that I might only know
Fulness of joy in everlasting flow.

Thine was the chastisement, with no release,
    That mine might be the peace;
The bruising and the cruel stripes were Thine,
    That healing might be mine;
Thine was the sentence and the condemnation,
Mine the acquittal and the full salvation.

For Thee revilings, and a mocking throng,
    For me the angel-song;
For Thee the frown, the hiding of God's face,
    For me His smile of grace;
Sorrows of hell and bitterest death for Thee,
And heaven and everlasting life for me.

Thy cross and passion, and Thy precious death,
    While I have mortal breath,
Shall be my spring of love and work and praise,
    The life of all my days;
Till all this mystery of love supreme
Be solved in glory—glory's endless theme.

Love for Love.

I John 4:16.

Knowing that the God on high,
    With a tender Father's grace,
Waits to hear your faintest cry,
    Waits to show a Father's face,—
Stay and think! — oh, should not you
Love this gracious Father too?

Knowing Christ was crucified,
    Knowing that He loves you now
Just as much as when He died
    With the thorns upon His brow,—
Stay and think! — oh, should not you
Love this blessèd Saviour too?

Knowing that a Spirit strives
    With your weary, wandering heart,
Who can change the restless lives,
    Pure and perfect peace impart,—
Stay and think! — oh, should not you
Love this loving Spirit too?

The Scripture cannot be broken.

John 10:35.

Upon the Word I rest,
    Each pilgrim day;
This golden staff is best
    For all the way.
What Jesus Christ hath spoken,
    Cannot be broken !

Upon the Word I rest,
　　So strong, so sure,
So full of comfort blest,
　　So sweet, so pure !
The charter of salvation,
　　Faith's broad foundation.

Upon the Word I stand !
　　That cannot die !
Christ seals it in my hand.
　　He cannot lie !
The word that faileth never !
　　Abiding ever !

Chorus.　The Master hath said it !　Rejoicing in this,
　　We ask not for sign or for token;
His word is enough for our confident bliss,—
　　"The Scripture cannot be broken !"

"I Did This for Thee! What Hast Thou Done for Me?"

(Motto placed under a picture of our Saviour in the study of a German divine.)

I gave My life for thee,	Galatians 2:20.
My precious blood I shed,	1 Peter 1:19.
That thou might'st ransomed be,	Ephesians 1:7.
And quickened from the dead.	Ephesians 2:1.
I gave My life for thee;	Titus 2:14.
What hast thou given for Me?	John 21:15 –17.
I spent long years for thee	1 Timothy 1:15.
In weariness and woe,	Isaiah 53:3.
That an eternity	John 17:24.
Of joy thou mightest know.	John 16:22.
I spent long years for thee;	John 1:10,11.
Hast thou spent one for Me?	1 Peter 4:2.
My Father's home of light,	John 17:5.
My rainbow-circled throne,	Revelation 4:3.
I left, for earthly night,	Philippians 2:7.
For wanderings sad and lone.	Matthew 8:20.
I left it all for thee;	2 Corinthians 8:9.
Hast thou left aught for Me?	Luke 10:29.

I suffered much for thee,	Isaiah 53:5.
More than thy tongue may tell,	Matthew 26:39.
Of bitterest agony,	Luke 22:44.
To rescue thee from hell.	Romans 5:9.
I suffered much for thee;	1 Peter 2:21 –24.
What canst thou bear for Me?	Romans 8:17,18.
And I have brought to thee,	John 4:10,14.
Down from My home above,	John 3:13.
Salvation full and free,	Revelation 21:6.
My pardon and My love.	Acts 5:31.
Great gifts I brought to thee;	Psalm 68:18.
What hast thou brought to Me?	Romans 12:1.
Oh, let thy life be given,	Romans 6:13.
Thy years for Him be spent,	2 Corinthians 5:15.
World-fetters all be riven,	Philippians 3:8.
And joy with suffering blent;	1 Peter 4:13 –16.
I gave Myself for thee:	Ephesians 5:2.
Give thou thyself to Me!	Proverbs 23:26.

To Thee.

"Lord, to whom shall we go?"—John 6:68.

I bring my sins to Thee,
    The sins I cannot count,
That all may cleansèd be
    In Thy once opened Fount.
I bring them, Saviour, all to Thee,
The burden is too great for me.

My heart to Thee I bring,
    The heart I cannot read;
A faithless, wandering thing,
    An evil heart indeed.
I bring it, Saviour, now to Thee,
That fixed and faithful it may be.

To Thee I bring my care,
    The care I cannot flee;
Thou wilt not only share,
    But bear it all for me.

O loving Saviour, now to Thee
I bring the load that wearies me.

I bring my grief to Thee,
    The grief I cannot tell;
No words shall needed be,
    Thou knowest all so well.
I bring the sorrow laid on me,
O suffering Saviour, now to Thee.

My joys to Thee I bring,
    The joys Thy love hath given,
That each may be a wing
    To lift me nearer heaven.
I bring them, Saviour, all to Thee,
For Thou hast purchased all for me.

My life I bring to Thee,
    I would not be my own;
O Saviour, let me be
    Thine ever, Thine alone.
My heart, my life, my all I bring
To Thee, my Saviour and my King !

What Thou Wilt.

Do what Thou wilt! Yes, only do
    What seemeth good to Thee:
Thou art so loving, wise, and true,
    It must be best for me.

Send what Thou wilt; or beating shower,
    Soft dew, or brilliant sun;
Alike in still or stormy hour,
    My Lord, Thy will be done.

Teach what Thou wilt; and make me learn
    Each lesson full and sweet,
And deeper things of God discern
    While sitting at Thy feet.

Say what Thou wilt; and let each word
　　My quick obedience win;
Let loyalty and love be stirred
　　To deeper glow within.

Give what Thou wilt; for then I know
　　I shall be rich indeed;
My king rejoices to bestow
　　Supply for every need.

Take what Thou wilt, belovèd Lord,
　　For I have all in Thee!
My own exceeding great reward,
　　Thou, Thou Thyself shalt be!

Reality.

"Father, we know the REALITY of Jesus Christ."—
Words used by a workman in prayer

　　Reality, reality,
　Lord Jesus Christ, Thou art to me !
From the spectral mists and driving clouds,
From the shifting shadows and phantom crowds;
From unreal words and unreal lives,
Where truth with falsehood feebly strives;
From the passings away, the chance and change,
Flickerings, vanishings, swift and strange,
　　I turn to my glorious rest on Thee,
　　Who art the grand Reality.

　　Reality in greatest need,
　Lord Jesus Christ, Thou art indeed !
Is the pilot real, who alone can guide
The drifting ship through the midnight tide?
Is the lifeboat real, as it nears the wreck,
And the saved ones leap from the parting deck?
Is the haven real, where the barque may flee
From the autumn gales of the wild North Sea?
　　Reality indeed art Thou,
　　My Pilot, Lifeboat, Haven now !

Reality, reality,
In brightest days Thou art to me !
Thou art the sunshine of my mirth,
Thou art the heaven above my earth,
The spring of the love of all my heart,
And the Fountain of my song Thou art;
For dearer than the dearest now,
And better than the best, art Thou,
Belovèd Lord, in whom I see
Joy-giving, glad Reality.

Reality, reality,
Lord Jesus, Thou hast been to me.
When I thought the dream of life was past,
And "the Master's home-call" come at last;
When I thought I only had to wait
A little while at the Golden Gate,—
Only another day or two,
Till Thou Thyself shouldst bear me through,
How real Thy presence was to me,
How precious Thy Reality !

Reality, reality,
Lord Jesus Christ, Thou art to me !
Thy name is sweeter than songs of old,
Thy words are better than "most fine gold,"
Thy deeds are greater than hero-glory,
Thy life is grander than poet-story;
But Thou, Thyself, for aye the same,
Art more than words and life and name !
Thyself Thou has revealed to me,
In glorious Reality.

Reality, reality,
Lord Jesus Christ, is crowned in Thee.
In Thee is every type fulfilled,
In Thee is every yearning stilled
For perfect beauty, truth, and love;
For Thou art always far above
The grandest glimpse of our Ideal,
Yet more and more we know Thee real,
And marvel more and more to see
Thine infinite Reality.

Reality, reality
Of grace and glory dwells in Thee.
How real Thy mercy and Thy might !
How real Thy love, how real Thy light !
How real Thy truth and faithfulness !
How real Thy blessing when Thou dost bless !
How real Thy coming to dwell within !
How real the triumphs Thou dost win !
 Does not the loving and glowing heart
 Leap up to own how real Thou art?

Reality, reality !
 Such let our adoration be !
Father, we bless Thee with heart and voice,
For the wondrous grace of Thy sovereign choice,
That patiently, gently, sought us out
In the far-off land of death and doubt,
That drew us to Christ by the Spirit's might,
That opened our eyes to see the light
 That arose in strange reality,
 From the darkness falling on Calvary.

Reality, reality,
 Lord Jesus Christ, Thou art to me !
My glorious King, my Lord, my God,
Life is too short for half the laud,
For half the debt of praise I owe
For this blest knowledge, that "I know
The reality of Jesus Christ,"—
Unmeasured blessing, gift unpriced !
 Will I not praise Thee when I see
 In the long noon of Eternity,
 Unveiled, Thy "bright Reality !"

Eight Poems by Frances Ridley Havergal (1836–1879)

Index to First Lines of Poems.

STAY AND THINK.

Words and Music by
Frances Ridley Havergal

1.Know-ing that the God on high, With a ten - der Fa-ther's grace, Waits to hear your faint - est cry, Waits to show a Fa-ther's face:— Stay and Think! Stay and Think! Stay and Think! Stay and Think! How He loves!__ Oh, should not__ you Love this__ gra - cious Fa - ther too?

2. Knowing Christ was crucified,
  Knowing that He loves you now
Just as much as when He died
  With the thorns upon His brow,—
Stay and think! — oh, should not you
Love this blessèd Saviour too?

3. Knowing that a Spirit strives
  With your weary, wandering heart,
Who can change the restless lives,
  Pure and perfect peace impart,—
Stay and think! — oh, should not you
Love this loving Spirit too?

www.ingramcontent.com/pod-product-compliance
Lightning Source LLC
Chambersburg PA
CBHW071820020426
42331CB00007B/1571